dixi
books

Solen KIPOZ

Solen Kipoz is an academic and designer working in the field of fashion studies. Since 2001 she has been an academic member of Department of Fashion and Textile Design at Izmir University of Economics where she has delivered courses on design studio, fashion theory and ethics and social responsibility in design. Associate Prof. Dr. Solen Kipoz produces publications on fashion studies and conceptual design works on ethical, social and sustainable fashion. Her book entitled *Sustainable Fashion* (2015) published in Turkish, has been influential in the path of creating an awareness on slow and ethical fashion in Turkey. Her personal exhibition *Ahimsa: The Other Life of Clothes* (2012), her installations and performances for Portizmir 3 International Contemporary Art Triennial (2014), *Asteya* (2017) and *Salvaged Leather* (2019) exhibitions are some of her notable works. The rag doll which can be produced and personalized by the user, which she designed as a part of the installation "The Legacy in the Pocket" is registered as a utility model by Turkish Patent Institute. Kipoz co-created this project with both women communities and children and teenagers.

SLOWNESS IN FASHION

SOLEN KIPOZ

Dixi Books
Copyright © 2020 by Solen Kipoz
Copyright © 2020 Dixi Books

Slowness in Fashion
Solen Kipoz
Cover Design: Carlotta Notaro
Designer: Pablo Ulyanov
Proofreading: Andrea Bailey
Printed by Mega Print
I. Edition: January 2020

Library of Congress Cataloging-in-Publication Data
Solen Kipoz- 1st ed.
ISBN: 978-619-7458-23-7
1. Ecology 2. Adult Non-Fiction 3. Fashion 4. Slow Fashion
5. Sustainable Fashion 6. Fashion Design 7. Design Ethics 8. Philosophy

© Dixi Books Publishing
20-22 Wenlock Road, London, England, N1 7GU
info@dixibooks.com
www.dixibooks.com

SLOWNESS IN FASHION

SOLEN KIPOZ

dixi
books

The Voice of the New Age

Contents

*F*oreword

Alison Gwilt

For the many people who lived in a pre-industrial Western society, clothes were amongst their most valuable possessions (Crane 2000). Cloth was often so expensive it was exchanged for payment in lieu of gold. Everyday life involved clothes being used and reused, pawned, sold and re-sold, bequeathed, and at the end of its wearable life, discarded and collected by the "ragpicker" to be used again. Historically then, cloth has always been a valuable commodity, but perceptions of material value was, and still is very different across society. As Strasser noted in respect to how waste materials are valued, the "...ones who perceive value are nearly always the ones with less money..." while the "...wealthy can afford to be wasteful." (1999, p.9).

The contemporary discourse around slow fashion resonates with this historical account of "valuable" clothes. There has been much discussion on how we should make clothes less transitory, more durable and longer lasting. However, these practical applications are only part of the story. Despite the many researchers and theorists who have argued that attitudes and behavior towards consumption needs to change, our machine-made fast fashion products allow people across the social divide to effortlessly consume clothes. Strasser's depiction of the perceptions of value and being wasteful has become somewhat blurred in contemporary society; clothes are now more accessible, cheaper and disposable and serve a wide range of distinct market levels. And too often through media saturated marketing the value in owning clothes has shifted from the value of the physical materials to the value of the brand.

However the "conscious citizen" is helping to motivate the fashion industry to change its practices, although solutions are often connected to encouraging "conscious consuming" - buying more - but "better" stuff. The conscious citizen demands that fashion brands become more transparent across their supply chain, less exploitative of workers and do better for the environment. And so the industry has to do much more. While our conscious citizens provide a beacon of hope for an alternate fashion system it is evident that the sale of new clothes is still on the rise. And as highlighted in the Ellen MacArthur Foundation's report (2017), of real concern is that clothing users are now wearing garments less often and keeping them for a shorter period of time. These points beg the question, how can we encourage people to resist the (over) consumption of clothes, and further, keep the clothes that they own in active use for as long as possible.

In introducing this book, Solen Kipoz asks whether slow fashion can become a distinctive characteristic in fashion production and design? Since we know that design decisions – good or bad - impact on the life of clothes it is not impossible to propose that slow principles could underpin the creation of all clothing types. How might the fashion system look then? As the earlier section notes the challenges are manifold. Although organisations around the world, such as the UK registered charity, Waste and Resources Action Programme (WRAP), are working with industry stakeholders and consumers to spread their collective knowledge in this area to widely support change, the impact of these efforts is still not apparent in the everyday life of producing and consuming clothes. These challenges for the fashion industry are examined within this book.

Additionally a timely range of perspectives and approaches are also presented that provide clues as to how the transition to slow may occur. Slowness in association with localism could, as Fuad-Luke suggests, provide a collaborative culture of fashion. Bringing together local and global communities to collectively unite for a slow fashion movement. Many of the authors, such as Clark, suggest slow thinking also needs to consider the relationships people have with their clothes, and examine how they are used. And whether, as Esculapio remarks, the designer can play a part in fostering positive material interactions. Clothes need to stimulate meaningful interactions with their users, for an increased active life; a garment should be "fit for purpose", desirable to consumers and developed for longevity (Gwilt and

Pal, 2017). Reflecting on Payne's scrutiny of aesthetic durability and disposability, it is clear that our clothes should be adaptable, evolving, almost "living" artifacts that do no harm and instead enrich the well-being of individuals, societies and the natural world. This vision require designers to play an active role in helping create a material and emotional value on which clothing users build meaningful relationships.

But who can afford to be slow, asks Otto von Busch. Frequently sustainability is perceived as a middle class pursuit. Strasser's point made earlier, clearly demonstrates how the impact of a social class divide is felt when it comes to the value of stuff, including clothes. The price of slow fashion products are often higher than "non-sustainable" items, largely to reflect the true cost of goods and labour involved in making high quality clothes. This means that frequently slow fashion garments are unaffordable to many people, although this is not always the case. Nonetheless the blame for the over consumption of clothes is often shifted towards low socio-economic communities as the main proponents of fast fashion, which is an unfounded assumption.

It would be good to remember that many people unavoidably live slowly, whether they wish to or not. Living on the margins of society with minimal income often forces an individual to keep clothing for much longer than anticipated. How will the documented shift to an older age demographic in many countries impact on the consumption cycle of clothes, for example. Slowness in fashion requires a deeper examination so that we may understand the challenges and opportunities for the fashion community - the fashion brands, manufacturers and retailers, the workers, the independent makers and producers, and the different clothing users. Kipoz and the contributing authors provide discussion and insight that, in Kipoz's words, offer the promise of a more humane, ethical and slow future.

PREFACE
Solen Kipoz

"There is a secret bond between slowness and memory,
between speed and forgetting... The degree of the slowness is
directly proportionate to the intensity of memory; the degree of
the speed to the intensity of forgetting."
Milan Kundera

For fashion, which propounds an ongoing change, "slowness"
has become a resistance to the change, an ethical stance paradigm.
So much so that, it has become the language and manner of an
attitude that is attentive, sensitive and liable to nature and human
at the expense of confronting "speed" which is the power of
fashion. Considering the fact that the biorythm of many living
creatures and phenomena of the nature is fast, speed in itself is
not actually something we need to always avoid. On the other
hand, we cannot ignore the fact that the concept of speed, like
many metabolisms and organisms in nature, is manipulated by a
human-centric perspective. In the end, the industrial revolution
and the technology are the tools of speed that have been developed
to facilitate or enrich human life. Besides, the relationship
between slowness and speed may create a contradiction between
the natural and the artificial, and as Kundera expresses, it also
creates a dichotomy between memory and forgetting, that is to
say between the past and the future. Will the intensity of speed in
nature be the same as the speed of technology, or will the speed in
the past be the same as in today or in the future? In this framework,
is "slowness in fashion" about trying to turn back to the speed of
fashion in the past?

Slowness in terms of sustainability and slowness in terms of
fashion's memory intersect at a point where the life of a garment
can be long. However, as the physical life cycle of a garment cannot
be reconciled with the life of fashion, no matter how durable

they are, old clothes remain outside the value chain formed by the economic logic of fashion, or in the best-case scenario they are preserved in museums as a part of material culture. Yet, until the capitalist system replaced use value with exchange value, the life cycle of a garment had been limited to its lifespan. Moreover, today the value of the fashion object, which does not only have a material existence but also has an imagery existence, is measured by a symbolic way.

So, what do we mean by the speed of fashion? Oscar Wilde, one of the co-founders of the aesthetic movement, predicted that the inclination of fashion towards change was driven in mid-19th century by seasonality, in a period when the phenomenon of fashion gave its first signals, when he said that "Fashion is a form of ugliness so intolerable that we have to alter it every six months." Indeed, as from 1970s , with the institutionalization of the industry in Western fashion, the fashion cycle required a designer to present a spring/summer, autumn/winter collection at least twice a year. With the globalization corresponding to 2000s, this number increased to four and/or six times a year; now only no more than a dozen high fashion - *haute couture* - fashion houses, offer two collections a year; all the other designers who are working with designer brands - *pret-e-porter* - prepare two other collections in addition to these two called "Resort" and "Pre-fall". Fast fashion brands that are making mass production in the ready to wear garment industry have increased this number to almost eight. While each of these seasons with the appearance of new fashion designs further enlivened with high-budget promotional campaigns tantalizes the consumer, the consumer who thinks they have caught up with the fashion suddenly realizes that the fashion has changed! The clothes in their wardrobe seem ugly, deficient and flawed without going through the physical aging process and these clothes which are put into the process of "artificial obsolescence" by the industry are now turning into worn-out-clothes to be discarded.

In this cycle, we may realize that the garment that is presented to us as "new" is not actually an innovative design which gives a fresh new idea, function or form, rather, a new garment is a product that has gone through a change with slight differences from the original, in details like colour, fabric, rather, cup, length. A fashion sociologist, Fred Davis (1992) likens the fashion cycle to a sea wave. Thus, as one wave disappears, it is replaced by a new one and so fashion, too, keeps waving. On the other hand, it is almost impossible for each individual of the society to keep up with the speed of changes in fashion. At this point, fast fashion confronts us with two different characteristics; first with its characteristic of providing fashion in a cheap and effective way to an audience with limited access to fashion innovations, that is to say democratizing fashion, and secondly with its characteristic of excluding the working classes subjected to modern slavery whose living conditions would never allow them to afford even the cost of cheap clothing. Furthermore, the effects of such fast and cheap fashion production are added to this cost (global warming, release of toxic chemicals, depletion of natural resources and non-biodegradable textile waste, etc.).

Thus, while fast fashion proceeds on its way at full speed, a handful of idealists on the planet has embarked on a quest so as to find an answer to the question "Is it possible to slow down this cycle?" Of course, we should not consider this as an approach that is about leaving fashion idle, stagnant and inertial, or trying to destroy fashion by opposing it. Like most avant-garde and counter movements, this also aims to proceed on its way by adding the concept of "slowness" to fashion, by raising the question "Can slow fashion become the characteristic of fashion?" instead of stating "There can be slow design without fashion." In this context, professor of fashion studies Hazel Clark's question in 2008 was meaningful: "Is the combination of slow and fashion an oxymoron?... or a promise for the future?" What made me think, work, produce and write on this subject was, in fact, this question. My collective book *Sustainable Fashion* (2015), which was prepared to share the philosophy and process behind a series of designs I produced in order to search for the answer of this question was actually trying to find and answer to the question "Can fashion be sustainable?" The concept of "slow fashion", which I discovered as one of the possibilities of acting ethical and responsible, became a loadstar and a guide in that journey as well. In this framework, this book, which I wish to call *Slowness in Fashion*, produced a reading which uncovers the "slow fashion" paradigm. Yes, slow fashion is a guide and a tool for sustainability and it seems that we do not have much time to do something about it. However, I would like to underline that I take attach importance to the fact that this reading should have a more distant and objective character which abstains an admiration for the concept of "slow fashion" yet, glorifying "slowness". What is more, with the fact that "slow fashion" along with "slow food", "slow city", "slow design", is one of the shining stars of the last 15 years' fields of research and practice, I thought it is necessary to seek an answer to the question "Where does slow fashion stand today?"

In the light of these ideas, this book can be considered as a kind of "slow fashion update". Within this scope, the research texts of eleven valuable experts with critical and analytical perspectives who have mastered the entire corpus of sustainable and slow design/fashion with their ideas, productions and publications, have formed the book's field of knowledge and discourse. What gave rise to the discussion was the chapter named "Rethinking Slowtopia" of the design theorist Alaistair Fuad-Luke, who conceptualized slow design for the first time 15 years ago. Fuad-Luke provides an insight as to how this concept evolved since its emergence by relaying the development of the "slow" framework. With the question of whether slowness can be a utopia, he focuses on the diversity-oriented and pluralist mission of the slow movement of a utopian world. Additionally, he is analyzing how the Slowtopia might respond to the socio-technological changes in the fluid modernity of the global world that we live in. He discusses how the emphasis of slowness on locality can turn into a slow-diversifying solidarist and collaborative culture, and how the alternative economies of the Slowtopia will take form. This interdisciplinary text of Fuad-Luke designates the meeting points of the textile and fashion design field with other creative disciplines and sectors.

The question of why we should develop a path towards slowness requires a careful analysis of the dominant fashion system. At this point, textile engineer and journalist/blogger Irem Yanpar Cosdan, first of all warns us with her chapter "Sustainable Approaches in Fashion and Textile Supply Chain" that the sustainability trend also creates a consumption culture. She provides a framework that the truly sustainable process can be read by following all stages of the global supply chain in the fashion industry, and only through this way ethical and fair trade conditions can be achieved to improve the impact of production processes on people and on the environment. As I mentioned above, Hazel Clark updates on the possibility of "slow" and "fashion" coming together, which she questioned ten years after her first article, with the chapter "Slow+Fashion: A Revisited" in this book. A guide for many researchers who have focused on the subject since then, this paper of Clark's, along with the adaptation of the manifesto at the Slow Design Conference held in Italy in 2006 under the leadership of design theorist Ezio Manzini, presented the outline of slow fashion. This outline was focusing on the potential to create a transparent relationship by destroying hierarchies between designers, producers and consumers; on the possibility of reinterpreting local skills and crafts in contemporary designs to create local economies against the global; and on the fact that emotionally and physically lasting and durable designs can be created with environmentally-friendly materials. Clark, in this article, stresses these principles, but this time with the suggestion of a "slower" fashion sense, she enriches the examples of slow design by turning the route to New York City, where she lives. She also sheds light on the driving force of women in this field with her painstaking study of the body of literature of the past decade.

In his chapter "Positioning Emotionally Durable Fashion: A Practise-Based Approach", Alex Esculapio associates the relationship we have with clothes in terms of durability with "slowness" by the help of an exhibition of used clothes. The article also deals with how clothes as objects create different meanings and impressions in terms of time and space than our relationships with clothes in everyday life in the perspective of curating and exhibiting experience. A fashion academic working on sustainability, Duygu Atalay emphasizes in the chapter "Traces of Craft in Slow Fashion: Designers & Crafts(wo)men Associations" that clothes whose design, production and consumption are from different parts of the world are considered as "the homeless" of today's global fashion network. She suggests that this sense of

17

belonging was lost in clothes. This "loss of aura" as the Marxist thinker Walter Benjamin emphasized, can be gained by storytelling and memory and that this may be possible by slowing down the production process practicing craft. Emphasizing that the notion of value in the slow philosophy is evolving into the what is produced with hand work and carefulness and with manual labor; she points out that the craft highlights cooperation and co-creation as a resistance to global fashion, that the emotional and narrative attachment of the producer to what (s)he produces may bring a more ethical and responsible understanding against the alienation of the crafts(wo)man from the production which is caused by the industrial system.

The South African fashion historian and curator Erica de Greef in her chapter "Two Fashion Tales: Re-use as Memory Practice in South Africa" searches for the past traces of re-use and upcycling, which are adopted as design practices in the slow fashion movement, through the social and political memory of her country. For de Greef, memory is where the old meets the new; De Greef reads how traditional clothing in costume museums transform over time, and analyzes the collections of contemporary South African fashion designers which are based on memory practices reveal this. In her research, remembering emerges as a resistance to the memory that forgets. According to de Greef, pulling out what is in the past means stopping time by activating memory. Slowing down time at the level of renewal that occurs through upcycling, which can have the power to heal and recover from wounds of the past. Within this scope, she shows that upcycling in memory practice displaces and slows down fashion's linear time.

On the other hand, in the chapter named "Economy Models That Slow Down Fashion: Circular and Sharing Economy" which is written by me, I suggest, on the grounds that the environmental and social impacts of the linearity of the global fashion system which are destructive, not constructive, that a circular and sharing/solidarist/collaborative way of thinking and economic model have a structure that slows down, repairs and improves. In this context, the paper outlines the circular design system by shedding light the waste problem with an elaborate analysis of a life cycle of a fashion garment. Following the footsteps of H. D. Thoreau who struggled for the environmental problems and human rights in the United Nations of America and M. Gandhi , India's leader of independence , I draw attention as to what kind of a resource the principles of "economic competence" and "the lack of property" creates in today's sharing economy. Yet, an academician working on sustainability in the fashion industry, Alice Payne from Australia, with her chapter "Speed as the Distance Travelled in Time: Re-framing Fast and Slow Fashion in Australia", critically re-examines the "fast fashion" and "slow fashion" dichotomy through a dialectical reading of time and space; and stresses that we should be suspicious towards the unconditional and biased ethical definition of "slow fashion", which evolved as an antidote against the environmental and social impacts of "fast fashion". Payne, reminding us that speed is considered as an ethics of distance and time in the fashion world, suggests that reading the ethics of speed can be done through measured time (chronological) and real time (kairaological); and outlines an impartial ethical inquiry through the fast fashion chains in her country Australia with their slow, fast and distant, close relationships.

There are very few sources that delve into the position of sustainable and slow fashion in design education. Academicians Yuksel Sahin and Sanem Odabasi, who work in the field of fashion and textile design, cover this gap to some extent with their chapter "Approaches on Sustainability and Slow Fashion in Fashion Design Education". They discuss where issues such as sustainability, slowness, ethics and responsibility stand in fashion design education, and how the vision of education can be shaped within possibilities and limitations. They convey their in-depth interviews with educators working and producing on the subject by making the three researches that they conducted transparent. They emphasize the need to internalize the meanings of popular concepts such as sustainable fashion, slow fashion; and to treat "slowness" as a path to sustainability in the construction and implementation of educational methods. An academician working in the field of textile design and sustainability, Nesrin Turkmen, in her writing "Hedonic Fashion Consumption and the Illusion of Happiness: Can We Slow Down?", investigates whether a space for slow fashion can be opened with happiness-oriented designs against the hedonic consumption model, which is often identified with the fast fashion trend, by focusing on the consumption dimension of the subject. In the modern society, which ensures the continuity of consumption at the same rate as production in order to continue the capitalist system; Türkmen, who brought new expansions in terms of social and positive psychology studies to the act of consumption which is turning into an illusion of happiness, underlines the power of positive designs to change our consumption habits in the "happiness economy".

The last chapter in the book is "Politics of Time in Slow Design" of Otto von Busch, professor of fashion studies, who frames the concept of social justice in fashion with his studies and publications. The text deals with how equally the time of fashion is distributed among the members of society and between different societies. In this regard; Von Busch, who claims that the consumption patterns created by the temporality of fashion defined by the seasons lead to constant change and renewal of identities, emphasizes that the fashion mechanism that envisages unconditional change has an energy that creates discriminatory and social frictions rather than a balancing and unifying role in society. What Otto von Busch thinks is the role of slowness in the fashion system is that although slowness is a stable ethical orientation that ideally predicts sustainable growth against the destructive effects of fast fashion, it is a trend that must be reached and captured by individuals in society just like fast fashion. By triggering this debate with his question "Who can afford to be slow in today's society?", he reminds us that the slow time is also a policy, pointing out that all individuals have access to the "speed of slowness" as a sign of political power. These remarks of Von Busch, who reminds us that slow fashion has an elitist and cliquey side in an ethical discourse like high fashion with the question "At this point then who will hit it?", brings to mind the question that "Should we progress by criticizing slow fashion while we build it?"

In line with these ideas, the second part of our book "Slowness in Fashion " gives a place to design and brand stories from Turkey and to the collectives and platforms acting in a social network. The design and brand examples discussed in this selection have focused on sustainability since their formation in terms of the resulting works and the characters of their creators and considering that the fashion industry has spread to a wide area of specialization, clothing designs are considered as paradigms to demonstrate fashion, other productions such as accessories and home textiles were excluded. The distinction between artistic and experimental design examples, and commercial and professional design activity has been drawn as design exhibitions and slow fashion brands. The selection is based on the design approach and design solutions that address the problems mentioned in the book in a design system. Three design exhibitions in this context belong to fashion academicians; these are "Seamless Clothes" by Sedef Acar, "Un-cut Clothes" by Yuksel Sahin and "Waste free Clothes" by Solen Kipoz. On the other hand, in the selection of slow fashion brands, we can talk about a very young and new formation with the exception of two or three examples. These brands adopt a boutique production model with a limited number of production and works in collaboration with a few experts in workshop environment, which has not engaged in any corporate promotional activity for communication or could not enter for economic reasons. They also have a special aesthetic taste and a sensitive ethical approach and creates a small economy compared to the dominant luxury and apparel industry. These brands are respectively; *Selçuki&Ali*, created by Selçuk Gürışık and Ali Alev by interpreting the felt craft with wearable artistic aesthetics; Gönül Paksoy, which interprets the upcycling technique with the collage aesthetics of fabrics that have historical value; *INCOMPLIT*, founded by Öykü Özgencil, which creates wearable examples of participatory and collaborative design, often producing together with disadvantaged children's communities; *Mandalinarossa*, a solidarist design brand that inspires the use of do-it-yourself model, the result of Nazlı Çetiner Serinkaya's journey which started with hand-knitted sweaters and continued with multi-functional clothes for children; *Reflect* founded by Edipcan Yıldız, Ece Altunmaral and Eray Erdoğan, which tells stories about social and global issues through designs, by being attentive to the transparency of production processes; *Sat-su-ma*, developed by Özge Horasan which fashions the vegetable dyed clothes with a simple aesthetic; *Argande*, a non-profit social responsibility brand supported by the United Nations Social Impact Fund, launched under the design directorship of the designer Hatice Gökçe; and *Zero Design* by Gülin Ölçer, which adopts the circular economy model as a design principle and provides waste management consultancy to companies.

Civil and independent activist platforms and collectives, which inform individuals and designers about sustainable production, consumption and communication models beyond design and production activities and which also urges solidarity, have an instrumental role in the formation and development of a sustainable and possible slow fashion culture. I also shared in this book such formations that are connected to a part of the international network in Turkey: there are respectively Clothing Swap, established by Nazlı Ödevci, which organizes free swap renewal markets and exchange events; CURCUIT Istanbul, organized by Ülkü Çağlayan, organizes collective art and cultural events for Sustainable Living; Turkey branch of international platform Fashion Revolution coordinated by Eda Çakmak, which was founded in order to raise awareness for environmental ethics and social problems and to call for action in fashion industry; Clean Clothes Campaign Turkey which is coordinated by Abdulhalim Demir (Bego), which focuses on improving the working conditions of workers in the fashion industry; and Sustainable Fashion Platform, which is a very new formation, encompassing the founders of almost all the slow fashion brands above.

In addition, I believe that the illustrations created by the designer and academician Kardelen Aysel by reading all the chapters and working in collaboration with me will enrich the texts visually as well as transform the reading action into a pleasant and ironic experience. I would like to thank all the authors , designers, brand owners and founders and members of the civil and independent communities who contributed to the formation of this book, the editors and the creative team of Dixi Books Publishing that I feel to be a part of. I am also grateful to Alison Gwilt, professor of ethical fashion studies, for her valuable contribution to the book with the preface. I hope "Slowness in Fashion" reaches different readers, whether they are interested in fashion or not; and I hope that it prompts and multiplies responsible, responsive and creative thinking and spreads the seeds of thought, which is the first step in changing, transforming and improving things.

Figure 1. Slowtopia (e.n.). Design and Illustration: Kardelen Aysel

Rethinking Slowtopia
Alastair Fuad-Luke

Opening threads

Slow and slowness were buzzwords in the early 2000s, possibly a symptom of an early millennium optimism that we could envisage different kinds of slower, more sustainable and rewarding kinds of living, production and consumption. Since then, the expansion of the internet, mobile telephony and online shopping has revolutionized people's consumption habits, further distanced consumers from the realities of production and enabled global economic growth. While Slow Food and Slow Cities (Citta Slow) have expanded their global reach, other initiatives of the slow movement, such as slow fashion and textiles remain active but diffuse. It is timely, therefore, to rethink Slowtopia in the age of instantaneity. As a foil to rethinking Slowtopia, this text examines some philosophical concepts, the potential of alternative economic models, our notions of diversity and the hidden potential therein.

The eutopias of slowness

Utopian rhetoric is a feature of many social, cultural and political movements. More kindly phrased, such movements have a dream envisioning better worlds through creating a new social imaginary. Such is the (pluralistic) vision of the slow movement best known through the activities of Slow Food and Slow Cities. Key values supporting the vision include authentic, local, fair and ecologically conscious production and consumption, respect for encultured and embedded knowledge and taking a long-term rather than short-term view. This requires a commitment to the integration of social networks and the agency of collective action locally by valueing the genius loci, by caring for place. In this sense, the slow movement is aiming for eutopias, ideal places of well-being. This rationale works well for locally produced food, maintaining the cultural heritage of small towns or cities, or local experiences described as slow travel, where the supply chain is short or it involves face-to-face exchanges. However, it becomes more problematic when we consider examples of slow design, such as slow fashion, where producer and consumer do not necessarily share the same place and where recalcitrant mainstream producer industries dominate the marketplace. Furthermore, the challenges facing the slow movement and slow design have undergone some seismic shifts in the last decade with the rapid global spread of mobile phone ownership and connection to the internet. As more of the underconsumers join the overconsumers by aspiring to their resource intensive Western/Northern lifestyles (Fuad-Luke, 2009) amplified by the reach of the internet, the juggernaut of neoliberal global capitalism accelerates. This acceleration is underlain with instantaneity identified by postmodern sociologist and philosopher Zygmunt Bauman as a key feature of liquid modernity, "the growing conviction that change is the only permanence and uncertainty the only certainty" (Bauman, 2000: p.8). Perhaps the notion of slowed up or ecological time that Anne Cline, a professor of architecture, called "nourishing rituals of delay" (Cline, 1998) simply cannot compete with the reality of always on, connected and stimulated. How has Slowtopia responded to these dramatic socio-technical changes?

Reflecting on Slowtopia

The slow movement began in the 1980s as a response to the internationalization of "fast food" global brands. Activist journalist Carlo Petrini's objection to a McDonalds restaurant in Rome set off a chain of events that led to the formation of Slow Food in 1989, still seen as emblematic of the slow movement itself. Slow Food's strategic impulse has been to focus the relationship between tradition and care of people and place. It is clearly an appealing story as the organization is represented in over 160 countries worldwide through 1,500 convivial or local chapters. Food must be good, clean and fair; its production contests large-scale intensive agricultural production through emphasizing appropriate small-scale farming and food production in social, environmental and economic terms; it is centred on the local as community and natural place; and time and passion are invested in a slow approach to gaining food quality (Tencati and Zsolnai, 2012). Slow Food also protects and nurtures encultured and embedded knowledge as valued means of production. This too seems to be the spirit of the Slow Cities charter with a focus on the production and consumption of local food, promoting local distinctiveness through commitment to conservation of the built environment, recognition of seasonality, traditional rhythms of community life and commitments to ISO9000 and ISO14000 focusing on environmentally managed production (Knox, 2005). While Slow Cities remains predominantly an Italian movement with 87 cities affiliated, and with strong representation in Western Europe, presently 236 cities are members globally. Both Slow Food and Slow Cities are pivotal in keeping the slow movement in the public eye. Both organisations promote their brands through conventional web and social media tools.

The situation is somewhat different when we turn to other domains of positive slowness. Slow fashion is driven by loose networks of independent freelance designers and collectives, fashion design researchers and fashion writers. It articulates a broad set of values around fiber and clothes production that shorten, and/or make transparent, clean and fair supply chains, that encourage producers to cooperate, that maintain local knowledge, skills and traditions, and that encourage extending the lifespan of clothing and/or encourage end-of-life reuse (see, for example, Clark, 2008; Fletcher and Grose, 2012; Kipoz, 2013). Slow fashion lacks a key international organization or organizational structures to gather around like Slow Food or Slow Cities, it is therefore a diffuse part of the slow movement with a difficulty to grasp identity or brand for producers and consumers alike. Furthermore, it is constantly plagued by a genuine conundrum affecting the mainstream fashion market - is it affordable, is it a ploy for market differentiation, etc.?[1]

Similarly, slow design has struggled to gain a genuine global dialogue remaining largely confined within the subfield of design research where most case studies are found – see for example, Local Wisdom (Fletcher, 2009-2018), the application of slow design principles to consumer products (Grosse-Hering et al, 2013), or the activities of the Slow Research Lab (Rais & Strauss,

27

2016). The Slow Research Lab focuses on slow design thinking as a way of exploring relationships within the self, with the collective, and with other-than-humans as a means to achieve a deeper philosophical and ecological understanding of the world. The speculative and fabulative practices discussed, originating from arts, design and hybrid epistemologies, can inspire individual creative practitioners and researchers, yet one wonders if, and how, these articulations reach a wider audience.

Slowness in our liquid modernity

Since slow design was first conceptualised fifteen years ago (Fuad-Luke, 2002) over half of humanity has been connected to the internet. Internet usage has risen from an average of 10 users per 100 inhabitants in 2002, to 23 by 2008 and 48 by 2017 – averaging 81 in so-called "developed countries" and 41 in "developing countries" (Ogden and Scarborough, 2017).[2] The hegemonic condition for half of humanity is liquid modernity (Bauman, 2000), bombarded by rapidly changing "images of thought" (Hroch, 2016). People may be simultaneously enlightened, educated, inspired, manipulated, seduced, pacified, numbed or marginalised. Who controls the content and flow of realities via the internet has considerable impact on aesthetical life experience where real and virtual worlds are seamless. In 2000 Will Murray, a brand strategist, projected this as the "intelligence economy" where the boundaries between natural and artificial intelligence are blurred (Murray, 2000). Perhaps we are still able to press the pause button on this possible dystopian future but there are some warning signs we should note. The technological capabilities being used by those wishing to manipulate our images of thought was recently demonstrated in a study of the spread of fake news and its ability to be amplified across media systems (Cadwalladr, 2016). Here openness, freedoms, rights and responsibilities tussle with a world of Black Transparency (MetaHaven, 2015) where accurate representation and truthfulness are relative, shifting, unpredictable, manipulated or absent. How in these contingent realities can Slowtopia be manifest?

Challenging Slowtopia through philosophical concepts

The main adversary of the slow movement can be clearly identified by taking a philosophical concept developed by the psychologist and philosopher Félix Guattari. He identified Integrated World Capitalism (IWC) as post-capitalism that is "delocalized and deterritorialised to such an extent that it is impossible to locate the source of its power" (Guattari [1989], 2000: p.4). Today, we recognise IWC as neoliberal global capitalism. He proposed ecosophy as a conceptual model to counter IWC. Ecosophy advocates the urgent development of new mental ecologies (our individual psyche), the rebuilding of the socius (where we collectivise our thoughts and actions), and the revitalization of our concern for the dynamics in our environment (Guattari, 1989, 2000). This remains consistent with the early conceptualisation of slow design to (re-)balance individual, social and environmental well-being (Fuad-Luke, 2002) and to challenge the narrow anthropological perspective of the global neo-liberal economic models that define everyone as customers (Fuad-Luke, 2002, 2008). Philosopher Jacques Rancière offers another useful concept for slow design whereby aesthetics is described as "the distribution of the sensible that determines a mode of articulation between forms of action, production, perception and thought" (Rancière 2000, 2013: p.86). It aligns well with design theorist and educator Alain Findeli's new paradigm for design education cited in the original conceptualization of slow design (Findeli 2001 cited in Fuad-Luke, 2002) although Rancière adds the critical element of production. Findeli argued that the current design paradigm, based upon "its materialistic underlying metaphysics; its positivistic methods of inquiry; and its agnosticist, dualistic worldview" (Findeli, 2001:p.5) – everyone is classified as consumers - was changing. He proposed a new logical structure of the design process where problem was replaced by state A of the system; solution by state B of the system; and the designer and user (stakeholders) are part of the system. His model requires an understanding of the underlying problématique of the social, economic, symbolic, political issues, placing perception and action, rather than science and technology, at the heart of his ethical design educational model. This is where designers can engage through, for example, design activism (Fuad-Luke, 2009; Thorpe, 2012) and its disruptive aesthetics (Markussen, 2013) and/or through product aesthetics as a means to challenge discourse (Folkmann, 2013: p.64). How we experience the sensible, the aestheticisation of life, affects how we experience being in life and, hence, what we can do and might or should do next. In order to challenge the dominant aesthetic regime, in this case IWC, we have to think, perceive, act and produce differently.

The alternative economies of Slowtopia

Many advocates of the slow movement stress the importance of creating new relationships in local economies that help build new social fabric while ensuring the vitality of existing socio-cultural structures. In effect, they advocate new models for alternative economies. It is here, perhaps, we have an opportunity to encourage new actions towards Slowtopia.

Recently, economist Kate Raworth noted that economists need new visualisations of alternative economies to replace those that support mainstream classical and neoliberal economic theory (Raworth, 2017). Fashion researchers Hirscher and Fuad-Luke (2013) asked how alternative modes of fashion production might challenge or fit with traditional and neoliberal, transitional or alternative exchange economies (Figure 1.1.). Clearly, there are synergies between the transitional and alternative exchange economies and the slow movement's values, aims and objectives and the socio-economic models they support. The common denominator is that new modes of production consider monetary and/or non-monetary, or a hybrid system of exchanges. Furthermore, many contributors in the Slow Reader (Pais & Strauss, 2016) stress the importance of building relationships for new types of exchanges, with different forms of collective governance signaling a desire to move beyond existing socio-economic constructs. Perhaps, then, slow design is in a unique position to amplify these alternative exchange economies to generate fresh narratives.

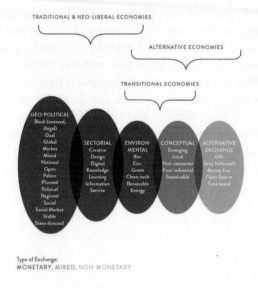

Figure 1.1. Traditional, neoliberal, transitional and alternative economies – which one is your fashion design supporting? (Hirscher and Fuad-Luke, 2013).

The question then, is what kinds of economies might we wish to catalyse, amplify or generally assist to elicit their becoming? These economies must deliver personal and collective well-being at the same time as delivering well-being for humans and other lifeforms, that is, they must be underpinned by ecosophical concerns. Today, there is an increased urgency as reports by the Intergovernmental Science-Policy Platform for Biodiversity and Ecosystem Services (IPBES) continue to show cataclysmic declines in biodiversity driven by our industrial and agricultural production systems, urbanization and land abandonment (IPBES, 2018). How can we, designers and others-as-designers (re-)make the world with improved bio-equity i.e. with more harmonious, synergistic relationships between humans and other lifeforms? Can slow fashion and slow textiles demonstrate how best to balance production with increasing bio-diversity?

Towards a Slowversity?

We have to examine more closely the concept of bio-diversity especially in regard to clothing and textiles made from natural fibres produced through agricultural activities or harvested from natural habitats. In a new project, entitled "What Could A Farm Be?" centred in the South Tyrol region of Italy, a new conceptual schematic of diversity, The Diversity Triangle, considers three overlapping elements of diversity: anthro-diversity which is the sum of linguistic, cultural, ethnic and other human-versities; Agro-diversity which focuses on the diversity in domesticated fungi, plants and animals; and bio-diversity which refers to all other living organisms found in human-made, semi-natural and natural habitats (Figure 1.2).

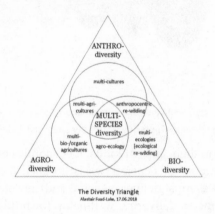

The Diversity Triangle
Alastair Fuad-Luke, 17.06.2018

Figure 1.2. The Diversity Triangle, presented at a workshop at Aspmayrhof, Val Sarentino, South Tyrol, Italy on 23 June 2018, https://diversescape.wordpress.com/2018/06/30/learning-from-exploration-01

The Diversity Triangle encourages us to think about the production, harvesting or hunting of natural fibres at the intersection of these diversities. In the centre of the venn circles, where these diversities meet, we arrive at multispecies diversity, a concept explored by Donna Haraway - the renown scholar in science and technology studies, ecofeminism and post-humanism - as a means to make new kinships (Haraway, 2016). The Diversity Triangle poses new challenges and opportunities for slow fashion and slow textiles. How does the cultural production of fibres link anthro-diversity with either agro-diversity (e.g. through the preservation and cultivation of heritage fibres) or bio-diversity (e.g. through the harvesting or hunting of fibres where the knowledge to do so is being lost)?

In seeking new sites of engagement and action for slow design, we should also re-examine opportunities through our daily activities. What if everyone had to grow plants, raise animals, nourish fungi and care for the fertility of soil? This was exactly Thomas More's proposition in Utopia (More, [1516] 1965). In this daring, and still relevant, narrative published in 1516, he sketched the daily life in Utopia[3] where everyone from the towns had to work two years in the countryside as a means to secure stable food production. Everyone developed personal and collective knowledge about this crucial activity. How might this work today? Civic land divided into small parcels or allotments, small urban agriculture schemes, community gardens, community supported agriculture (CSA) and other schemes such as edible estates or guerilla gardening already provide, on a limited scale, these kinds of activities (Fuad-Luke, 2017). Certainly the experiences within Alternative and Civic Food Networks (AFNs, CFNs) reveal opportunities for designers to amplify existing practices, especially if linked to ideas of local co-production. We need to look to the land to develop a notion of reciprocal care between humans and other lifeforms at a micro scale. What if we all had access to individual and/or collectively managed pieces of land? Here we could balance growing food, flowers, fibre or skins for clothing, or other raw materials, with providing a refuge or home for other-than-humans. A new generation of Slowtopian gardeners and farmers could refresh the visions of the slow movement, slow design and a life well-lived, not just for autonomous, bio- or organic food production but for collective fibre, animal and other by-products. In this vision we move beyond the narrow anthropology of IWC's customers to the author of "The Third Wave" Alvin Toffler's notion of prosumers, the producer-consumers (Toffler, 1971).

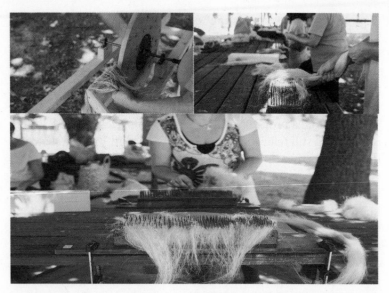

Figure 1.3. Alice Bernardo of Saber Fazer is teaching a newly urbanized generation how to grow for the production of linen. How to grow cannabis for the production of linen.

These Slowtopian visions might seem unrealistic, but actually exist in past and present design narratives. In 1995 architect and designer Andrea Branzi and colleagues proposed dynamic spatial arrangements of peri-urban, peri-rural situations with a mosaic of mixed land use (Branzi et al., 1995). Andre Viljoen, a professor of architecture at Brighton University, UK, coined the term Continuous Productive Urban Landscapes, CPUL (Viljoen, 2005). CPUL and other contemporary examples of urban and peri-urban agriculture demonstrate a desire for urban populations to engage with the land through the activity of growing their food. Can we extend these visions to include new modes of fibre and furniture production? Yes, because designers are already collaborating with diverse stakeholders to test these possibilities (Figure 1.3.).

Figure 1.4. Campo Libro which was established by Andrea Sebastianelli in Italy promotes a small-scaled production for for the manufacturing lines.

Campo Libro is a particularly relevant project as it proposes a small-scale localized system of production where farmers or organisations can hire or buy a modified machine for processing fibre in-situ and can link to a network of skilled craftspeople, designers and semi-skilled workers to generate unique products (Figure 1.4.) (Sebastianelli, 2017). The flexibility of the Campo Libro system potentially offers a revival of Italy's high quality historic hemp production and could potentially be applied to other fibres, such as nettles (Urtica species) also formerly grown in the region.

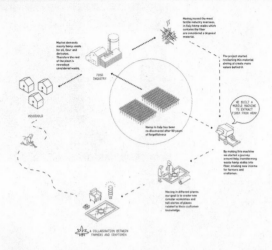

Figure 1.5. Campo Libro by Andrea Sebastianelli, 2017, a small-scale localized system of hemp fibre processing and unique product production.

Can these exploratory projects suggest new modes of local production for materials and commodities? If we really want to create slow gardens and slow farms as new centres of production then who owns the land and who has (legal) tenure, i.e. the rights to be on and work the land are critical issues. What kind of rights, including common rights, would we have to the land? Would we give rights to other living creatures? Given stable and fair tenure how might the land, and the people who work with it, generate new long-term relationships? How might we envision individual and shared or collective, slow production through models of commoning?

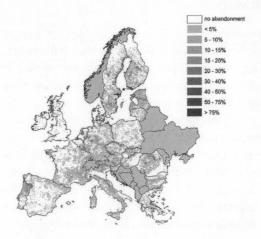

Figure 1.6. Localization of the hotspots of abandonment and rewilding in Europe. Those hotspots are areas categorized as "agriculture" in 2000 that are projected to become rewilded or afforested in 2030 and that are common to all four scenarios of the CLUE (the Conversion of Land Use and its Effects) model (Verburg and Overmars 2009) cited in Pereira and Navarro (eds) (2015), p11.

Can we mix these new modes of production, with rewilding our landscapes? Rewilding is a process of active and passive management encouraging species to return to areas where they were formally indigenous (Pereira and Navarro, 2015). Abandonment of farmland especially in southern, Mediterranean Europe offers an opportunity to extend rewilding (Figure 1.6). Abandoned farmland could also be opened up for experiments developing sustainable local fibre production economies, either through small-scale planting or harvesting wild fibres. This seems an opportunity to bring others into the slow design dialogue, such as farmers, rural development and ecological experts, rural entrepreneurs and citizens. Can slow gardens, slow farms and slow (co-)production help nurture "slowversity", i.e. positive slowness through symbiotic forms of production that maintain or enhance our diversities? Can we obtain fibres from a mixture of cultivated and wild biomass? This is an enormous challenge in a world where the liquid modernity of IWC continues rapid expansion. Perhaps, slow fashion and slow textiles through new modes of slow fibre production can show the way.

End-threads

Re-engagement of the slow fashion and texiles movement in the cultural, agri-cultural and wild production of fibres offers a means to revitalize conversations about how we make, who makes and who benefits (humans and other-than-humans). Of equal importance is how these stories are mediated, how we can engage the prosumers and how this can become a globalized system of local production networks. If Slowtopia is to gain critical attention then those interested in the future of slow fashion and textiles need to consider rethinking their clothing life cycle all the way back to the land, back to the soil, back to the roots. All the disparate actors should join their local or international initiatives under an umbrella organization that can act as a recognizable brand that is truly (micro-)local yet global, that links with small growers, farmers and urban farming communities. This organization could have a mobile phone app that allows you to locate your nearest production and the people behind it, i.e. Slowtopia in your locale, near you, accessible.

Bibliography

Bauman, Z. (2000) *Liquid Modernity*. Cambridge-UK, Polity Press.

Branzi, A., Donegani, D., Petrillo, A., Raimondo, C with David, T.B. (1995) Symbiotic metropolis. Agronica., in *The Solid Side. The search for consistency in a changing world. Projects and proposals*. Manzini, E. and Supani, M. (eds) The Netherlands: V&K Publishing with Philips Corporate Design and the Domus Academy, pp. 103-120.

Clark, H. (2008) Slow+Fashion an Oxymoron or a Promise for the Future...?. Fashion Theory, Vol. 12, issue, 4, pp. 427-466. Berg Publishers.

Cadwalladr, C. (2016) Google, democracy and the truth about internet search, The Guardian, 4th December 2016, https://www.theguardian.com/technology/2016/dec/04/google-de¬mocracy-truth-internet-search-facebook, [Accessed 22 March 2017]. Photograph: Jonathan Albright.

Cline, A. (1998) A Hut of One's Own – *Life Outside the Circle of Architecture*. Cambridge-MA, MIT Press.

Fletcher, K. (2009-2018) Local Wisdom. http://localwisdom.info/about, [Accessed 23 May 2018]

Fletcher, K. and Grose, L. (2012) *Fashion and Sustainability: Design for Change*. London, Lawrence King.

Findeli, A. (2001) Rethinking Design Education for the 21st Century: Theoretical Methodological and Ethical Discussion, Design Issues, Vol. 17, Number 1, Winter 2001, pp. 5-17.

Folkmann, M. N. (2013) *The Aesthetics of Imagination in Design*. Cambridge-MA, The MIT Press.

Fuad-Luke, A. (2002) *"Slow design – a paradigm shift in design philosophy?"*, a paper presented at the conference *Development by Design* (dyd02), Bangalore, India organized by MIT ThinkCycle.24

Fuad-Luke, A. (2008) *"Slow Design" in Design Dictionary: Perspectives on Design Terminology*. Erlhoff, M and Marshall, T. (eds). Basel, Birkhäuser Verlag.

Fuad-Luke, A. (2009) *Design Activism. Beautiful strangeness for a sustainable world*. London, Earthscan.

Fuad-Luke, A. (2017) An ecosophical inquiry into digital mediation and design in relation to Alternative Food Networks (AFNs) in an "expanded field" of "agri-culture". *Estudos em Comunicação*, No. 25, (2), pp. 35-60.

Grosse-Hering, B., Mason, J., Aliakseyeu, D., Bakker, C. and Desmet, P. (2013) "Slow Design for Meaningful Interactions". CHI 2013: Changing Perspectives, Paris, France, April 27 – May 2.

Guattari, F. (1989, 2000) *The Three Ecologies*. (Ian Pindar and Paul Sutton, Trans.), London, Bloomsbury Academic.

Haraway, Donna. (2016) *Staying with the Trouble. Making Kin in the Chthulucene*. Durham and London, Duke University Press.

Hirscher, A-L. & Fuad-Luke, A. (2013) "Open participatory designing for an alternative fashion economy", pp. 172-197, in Niin¬imäki, K. ed., *Sustainable Fashion: New approaches*, Helsinki- Finland, Aalto ARTS Books.

Hroch, P. (2016) Sustainable Design Activism: Affirmative Politics and Fruitful Futures, in *Deleuze and Design*, Marenko, B. and Brasset, J. (eds), Edinburgh, Edinburgh University Press, pp.219-245.

Intergovernmental Science-Policy Platform for Biodiversity and Ecosystem Services (IPBES), (2018) Summary for policymakers of the regional assessment report on biodiversity and ecosystem services for Europe and Central Asia of the Intergovern¬mental Science-Policy Platform on Biodiversity and Ecosystem Services. M. Fischer, M. Rounsevell, A. Torre-Marin Rando, A. Mader, A. Church, M. Elbakidze, V. Elias, T. Hahn. P.A. Harrison, J. Hauck, B. Martín-López, I. Ring, C. Sandström, I. Sousa Pinto, P. Visconti, N.E. Zimmermann and M. Christie (eds). IPBES secretariat, Bonn, Germany.

Kipoz, S. (2013) Slow Fashion Ethics: Reproduction of Memory through Deconstruction. 10th European Academy of Design Conference – Crafting the Future, Gothenberg, Sweden, 17th-19th April 2013.

Knox, P. L. (2005) Creating Ordinary Places: Slow Cities in a Fast World. Journal of Urban Design, Vol. 10, No. 1, pp. 1-11, February 2005.

Markussen, T. (2013) The Disruptive Aesthetics of Design Activism: Enacting Design Between Art and Politics, Design Issues, Vol. 29, No. 1, pp. 38-50.

Metahaven, (2015) Black Transparency. *The Right to Know in the Age of Mass Surveillence*. Berlin: Sternberg Press. More, T. (1516, 1965) Utopia. London, Penguin Books.

Murray, W. (2000) *Brand Storm*. London, Financial Times/Prentice Hall.

Ogden, J. and Scarborough, J. (2017) "Internet users per 100 inhabitants 1997 to 2017", years on the x axis, number of users on the y axis, according to the International Telecommunication Union (ITU). Jeff Ogden and Jim Scarborough, created October 2017, CC BY-SA 3.0, Wikipedia, https://en.wikipedia.org/wiki/Global_Internet_usage#/media/File:Internet_users_per_100_inhabitants_ITU.svg, [Accessed 17 April 2018]

Pereira, H.M. and Navarro, L.M. (eds) (2015) *Rewilding European Landscapes*. Heidelberg, Springer Open.

Rais, A.P. and Strauss, C.F. eds. (2016) *Slow Reader. A resource for design thinking and practice*. Amsterdam, Valiz.

Rancière, J. (2000, 2013) *The Politics of Aesthetics*. London: Bloomsbury Academic (First published in France under the title Le Partage du sensible: Esthétique et politique, La Fabrique-Éditions, 2000).

Raworth, K. (2017) *Doughnut Economics. Seven Ways to Think Like a 21st-Century Economist*. London, Random House Business Books.26

Sebastianelli, A. (2017) *Campo Libero. Un'unita de trasformazione della fibra di canapa per la ricostuzioned della filiera a livelo locale*. Thesis presented for the Masters in

Eco-Social Design, Free University of Bozen-Bolzano, Italy.

Tencati, A. and Zsolnai, L. (2012) Collaborative Enterprise and Sustainability: The Case of Slow Food. *Jnl. Business Ethics*, 110, pp. 345-354.

Thorpe, A. (2012) *Architecture & Design versus Consumption. How Design Activism confronts growth*. London, Earthscan.

Toffler, A. (1971). *Future Shock*. London, Bantam.

Viljoen, A.(ed.) (2005) *Continuous Productive Urban Landscapes CPULs: designing urban agriculture for sustain-able cities*. Oxford, Architectural Press.

NOTES

1   See, for example, a 2017 article in the New York Times by Hadley Freeman, What is Slow Fashion? We explain. https://www.nytimes.com/2017/10/11/fashion/what-is-slow-fashion.html. This was the second hit on the first page of a search result on Google for "slow fashion movement", [Accessed 15 May 2018].

2   By 2017 there were 4.16 billion internet users (see Internet World Stats, 2017, https://www.internetworldstats.com/stats.htm, [Accessed 17 April 2018] in relation to an estimated global population in 2015 of 7.35 billion people (see United Nations, 2015, Estimated world population, 1950 to 2015 and projections to 2010. Source: United Nations, Department of Economic and Social Affairs, Population Division, 2017. https://esa.un.org/unpd/wpp/Graphs/Probabilistic/POP/TOT/, [Accessed 17 April 2018].

3   Utopia translates literally as "not-place".

Figure 2. United Nation Sustainabe Development Goals (e.n.).
Design and Illustration: Kardelen Aysel

Sustainable Approaches to Fashion and Textile Supply Chain

Irem Yanpar Cosdan

Introduction

In recent years, the term "sustainability" has often been circulated in the fashion world. It has become a new trend with increasing environmental and social awareness in the society, which has led many fashion brands to build their marketing strategies on this issue. Unfortunately, unlike the principle of sustainability which is "not to take anything non-renewable from the nature", these strategies are based on the idea of Green Consumption[1], promoting a different form of consumerism. The "eco- friendly" illusion created by the brands through their products legitimize the overconsumption of their customers by easing their conscience. Hence, the so-called race of "being conscious" does nothing but nullify the term "sustainability."

Sustainability in fashion aims at reducing the environmental effects of the industry and increasing its social benefits. This can be achieved not through a distorted view of consumption or tiny steps taken for show purposes only, but through radical changes where every step in the fashion supply chain is scrutinized and where the production and consumption are consciously slowed down. In order to do this, it is important to realize the real price that our planet and textile workers pay for fast fashion, discover the key problems in the supply chain and produce innovative solutions to them.

This chapter is written to analyze the environmental and social impacts of the fast fashion system imposed on the consumers and discuss what could be done with today's technology by following the supply chain step by step.

The price of fast fashion

The renewal pace of nature cannot catch up with our overconsumption anymore. Fashion industry is now defined by the concept of "fast fashion", in which "must wear clothes" change annually or even monthly. This system takes its power from the exploitation of resources and labor and has turned into a cycle from which big fashion brands make an incredible amount of profit.

The developing technology and mechanization have multiplied the speed of textile production. The introduction of synthetic textile fibers to our lives and the toxic artificial dyes with a wider color options reduced the costs and facilitated the production.

The system has evolved further with the emergence of cheap labor. It created an artificial perception of prosperity by providing a large number of low-priced products into the market. In this prosperity, consumers started to buy new clothing instead of, for example, fixing a broken button, simply because they thought it is not worth their time and efforts. However, today we see that the real price of the cheap garments are much higher than what is shown on the price tag, and that this price is stolen from the resources of our planet and the lives of textile workers. Fashion industry alone is responsible for 8% of the global climate change (ClimateWorks Foundation, 2018) and 4% of total waste with 92 million tons per year (Kerr and Landry, 2017). Each year, 60 out of 400 billion m^2 fabric produced for clothes is wasted just at the cutting stage (Chung, 2016). 20% of the fresh water pollution arises from textile dyeing and finishing processes (Ditty 2017, p.12). The excessive demand for leather, wool, fur, goose and rabbit feather as luxury items at high prices result in the slaughter and torture of millions of animals. Fashion brands neglect the ethical standards of the animal treatment for the sake of better output.

The fact that the process of sewing, namely apparel manufacturing, has not been fully automatized is the reason why fashion industry continues its labor-intensive structure. According to the 2015 report by the Clean Clothes Campaign, there are 75 million textile workers in the world, three-quarters of whom are women (Stotz and Kane, 2015). In Asian countries, where the production of textiles is very intense, wages of workers might fall to half of the living wage[2] (Kerr and Landry, 2017).

There are serious obstacles to sustainability in fashion industry which needs the cycle of production and consumption to be constantly renewed. The efforts of fast fashion brands to reduce the cost of their products, the overconsumption triggered by cheap and low-quality garments and long, non-transparent supply chains are the main obstacles to sustainability. When we get to the root of the problem, we see that it is not fashion itself, but it's speed of change. In other words, fashion is based on a system of fast and excessive consumption. The slow fashion movement aims at slowing down not only consumption but also the design and supply chain. It opens the way for a new era in the fashion industry as a source of inspiration for rational and innovative practices.

Designing stage: planning the impact

The impact of our garments on nature and people begins to take shape in the very first step of the supply chain, the design stage. The material, color and model that the designer chooses for the product directly affects how much water, energy and chemicals will be used in production. The life cycle of the product is determined by features such as the timelessness of the model, the durability of the stitch, the comfort and customizability it provides to the wearer. The duration of this period is one of the most important steps in slowing the fashion.

The main practices that greatly reduce the environmental impact of the product are the reuse of textile waste, choice of organic or recycled fabrics, techniques based on the principle of zero waste at the cutting stage, and sewing methods that ensure easy recycling of the product after its expiration.

The main components of slowing down both in the supply chain and consumption are planning every stage of production with sustainable design approach and aiming for the long duration of use with correct materials and techniques. At this point, it is necessary that designers to realize the power in their hands and take their decisions considering not only the cost and sale but also the environmental and social impacts of the product.

Material choice: eco-friendly materials

An important part of the environmental impact of the textile industry originates from the material choice.

The degree of its impact is determined by the acquisition of raw materials, the processes through which it becomes ready for use and the recyclability after use. It is known that synthetic fibers, which are mostly derived from petroleum, cause environmental damage. However, the natural content of the fiber, contrary to the common belief, is not enough to make it eco-friendly. Moreover, according to the "Higg Index" data developed by "Sustainable Apparel Coalition (SAC)"[3], which makes it possible for companies to measure their sustainability performance, revealed that some natural fibers such as cotton, wool and silk have more environmental impacts than other materials. The reason for this is the amount of water and chemicals used in their production as well as the greenhouse gases that cause global warming. For example, cotton, which is one of the most used textile fibers due to its comfort and maintenance, requires high amounts of water during its cultivation. It can take 2,700 liters to produce the cotton needed to make a single t-shirt. (WWF, 2013). Moreover, this amount increases when the other production steps are added. Also, the excessive use of pesticides during the cultivation of cotton reduces the rate of carbon and hence the productivity of the soil.

It can be said that no material used in the textile industry is completely sustainable, but some have a lower environmental impact than others. For instance, organic cotton, which requires less water than traditional cotton, does not have any adverse effects on the soil, farmer and the ecosystem in the cultivation area, as no pesticides are used in its production. In addition, natural fibers, such as linen and hemp, which require relatively less water and no pesticides, are much more eco-friendly, though their use is limited now.

Developing technology brought new materials to textile as well as other industries. The rapid depletion of limited resources led the studies in this field to focus on the evaluation of waste. Some of these are new-generation textile fibers such as orange (Orange Fiber, 2018), banana (Kaur, 2018) and pineapple leaves attained from agricultural waste (Pinatex, 2017). These promising and innovative studies offer new raw material options for the industry and hint at what we can do in the future.

Recycled material usage

Apart from eco-friendly and innovative materials, the use of recycled fibers continues to rise among the brands committed to sustainability. The use of recycled fibers in products aims at reducing the environmental damage by deactivating the acquisition and processing of raw materials taken from nature. However, when we look at the tag of the products indicating "produced from recycled fibre", we see that they include a very small proportion of those materials, as the rest includes traditional fibers, sometimes even more harmful to the environment. This, in turn, is an indication of how ethically(!) recycling in textiles is reflected to the final consumer.

The technical limitations of getting fiber from textile products through recycling make this process very difficult. Natural fibers can be recycled mechanically but this results in a significant reduction in quality, as it causes the shortening of the length of fibers. Chemical recycling of synthetic fibers such as polyester increases the use of chemicals in the production stage, although it gives better results in terms of fiber quality.

The recycling of textile materials that include more than one fiber is much more difficult and demanding. The cost of the process increases when details such as zipper, button and embroidery are used in the garments. A majority of recycled materials find their place in lower positions (down-cycling) than the first purpose of use. One of the most common examples is when a material previously used as a garment, is now used for insulation purposes in the construction industry after recycling.

Although recycling is a promising process, with a cost burden, its use and impact area are unfortunately very limited. Difficulties in operation, technical limitations and the discrepancy between the speed of recycling and consumption lead to question sustainability of the system. The way in which recycling can contribute to a fully closed-loop life cycle is through the development of technology and bringing the efficiency and costs to the optimum level. But no matter how much technology is developed, if our speed of consumption does not slow down, recycling will not be more than a green marketing strategy of brands.

Textile production: natural dyes

All of the processes including production of yarn and fabric out of textile fibers, their coloring and finishing processes can be analysed under the subject of textile production. Among these stages; dyeing and textile finishing processes play an important role in determining the environmental impacts of companies due to intensive water, energy and chemical use.

Until the mid 19th century, organic materials from plants, insects and minerals were used to color textile materials. Red color was extracted from cochineal insect or plant madder, blue color was extracted from indigo, and saffron was used to get the yellow color. With the discovery of the first synthetic dye mauveine in 1856, aniline dyes taken from coal began to replace the natural ones very quickly. The cost of synthetic dyes, which made it possible to obtain more vivid and lasting colors, was also advantageous. However, textile workers soon began to experience many health problems from skin irritation to intoxication. Another controversial synthetic colorant known for its cancerogenic effect, azo dye, even though prohibited in many places, is still being used by some producers due to its efficiency and fastness (Gordon and Hill, 2015: p. 110).

Toxic chemicals used in textile production, as a result of the lack of wastewater treatment process, interfuses with rivers and the drinking water of the people living in the surrounding neighborhood. Since 2011, The Greenpeace's detox campaign against the production, use and release of hazardous chemicals into the environment, urged many companies to take action on the issue (Greenpeace, 2017). In the areas where textile production is intense, Greenpeace has been taking samples from rivers and encountered many toxic chemicals, and later revealed the wrong practices of brands in a report. Even though it is not possible to follow all the production steps in long supply chains of these brands, which completely deceive their transparency, these types of public pressure are quite effective in terms of protecting the environment and the employees.

It is possible to reduce environmental impacts through building wastewater treatment plants according to standards, use of clean energy sources such as solar and wind energy and innovative production techniques that minimize water use. In addition to these practices, the studies on natural dyes, whose use is still being discussedon an industrial scale, continue at full speed. The need for a high amount of raw materials in the preparation of natural dyes led the studies in this field to focus on the use of agricultural waste. It is much easier to get rid of the excess dye from the material after the coloring process in vegetational dying, which primarily includes plants such as nut shell, tea and stinger in Turkey, rather than synthetic dyes. This means less water, less energy and lower use of chemicals.

Big companies still prefer synthetic colorants in their production mainly because there are difficulties in attaining the same color tone in natural dyeing. Chemicals that do not undergo an adequate purification process affect not only the environment in which the production is carried out, but also the whole ecosystem and people living in it. At this point, we should question the fast fashion system, which makes all of us wear the same color tone that soon will become obsolete, and realizing that all these harmful chemicals are used to make more profit, not to protect limited resources.

Garment production: making labor visible

Converting fabrics into finished products, i.e. garment production, has the biggest social impact in supply chain. This area, which is labour-intensive as it cannot totally be mechanized, is focused on countries such as Bangladesh, Vietnam, India and Cambodia due to cheap labor. People have to work in textile factories despite heavy conditions, because the gigantic textile production centers do not give any opportunity for another business area. The working conditions of clothing industry were at the center of public discussions when 1.134 people died and hundreds got injured in Bangladesh in 2013 at Rana Plaza Factory Collapse (Rana Plaza Factory Collapse History Cities 50 Buildings, 2015). This production center's continuing to work despite being reported as unsafe a few days ago before the accident, resulted in the loss of many lives. After the collapse, many NGOs and trade unions scrutinizing the working conditions of workers published various reports about the issue.

Figure 2.1. In supplier countries where labor force is cheap and working conditions are not controlled, sometimes the real price of fashion is paid with the lives of workers (e.n.). Design and Illustration: Kardelen Aysel

According to "Living Wage Now!" report in 2015 by Clean Clean Clothes Campaign, in Cambodia, textile workers are not even allowed to have a lunch break to maximize the productivity. They are working 12-14 hours a day, earning below the living wage defined by the Asia Floor Wage Alliance-Cambodia, as the minimum income necessary for a worker to meet their basic needs. (Crabbe, Wong & Yanz, 2015) Unfortunately, the situation is not very different in most countries producing textile and apparel. Every day, textile workers are facing with modern day slavery such as forced labor, discrimination and sexual harassment.

Big fashion brands, in order to end the child labor and the inhuman practices textile workers are exposed to, make their suppliers sign many code of conduct contracts, on the other hand, they keep on pressing hard to cut prices in order to reduce the cost.

Thus, while putting all the responsibility on their suppliers, in fact they indirectly lead them to exploit the labor force. However, in the age of communication, it is no longer possible for them to continue their operations in this way. The technology that enables us to witness simultaneously an event on the other end of the world, forces brands to be transparent as never before in their practices by creating a serious public pressure on them.

The platform "Fashion Revolution", seeking to create public opinion against brands on transparency, is one of the most important steps in this path. The nonprofit organization which was established after the Rana Plaza disaster, not only informs the customers about negative social impacts of fashion industry but also urges them to ask questions to brands on social media with the campaign "#whomademyclothes". It is an important indication of the consumers' power that already many brands are now responding to these questions.

The people who produce our garments can work in better conditions only if they are visible. Many fashion brands seeking to create social benefit share frequently the stories of their workers in their websites and social media channels. Thus, the human power and labor in the supply chain, differentiating from machines, meet the consumers. One of the best examples to this is California-centered Known Supply Brand (Known Supply Website, 2018), that put the name of the worker who had sewn that product on the fabric tags of their products.

Figure 2.2. Workers not appearing on the global network of mainstream fashion can be made visible by some brands that have ethical efforts. Drawn with inspiration from Known Supply website (e.n.). Design and Illustration: Kardelen Aysel.

Fast fashion system that takes into account even the seconds in the production processes, aims at getting the maximum number of products by measuring the worker performance. This speed and performance pressure cause low quality products and lead workers to do overtime. By slowing the system, this vicious circle that makes both producers and consumers unhappy can be broken. In a system that values handicraft and artisanship, benefits from cultural and local labor, leads women labor force to give the product identity and quality; the production will slow down and gain value and as a result the meaning given to the product will increase. Thus the products whose quality and value increase, will leave being a part of fast fashion and contribute to the social benefit by building a bridge between consumer and maker.

Sustainable distribution centers

Most of the brands which have international supply chains cooperate with professional and experienced companies for their logistic operations. In this way, they are able to reduce their environmental effects by benefiting from other industries' know-how without needing to spend resources for process improvement. At this point, every step ranging from the introduction of reusable cloth bags instead of paper or plastic to new generation logistic centers is crucial for the environmental impact of the industry.

One of the most extensive examples on this issue is the distribution center which is built by Nike in Belgium that uses totally renewable energy. Including wind turbines and solar panels, the center recycles 95% of the waste as a result of its operations. Thanks to its canal and railway, the carbon emission of within- center transportation is much lower than that of a motorway (Un Global Compact Website, 2017).

In global supply chain, evaluations that ignore carbon footprint and waste from packaging and transportation, no matter how much the products are eco-friendly, are insufficient. Here, brands need to do innovative studies on how they could reduce their environmental effect by analyzing their operations in detail.

A new period in sales and marketing: transparency

Under today's conditions in which we can get access to every product anytime, why we buy has become more important than what we buy. Brands have started to build their sales and marketing plans on selling not the product but lifestyle and experience. As phenomena such as global warming, limited resources reaching a level of extinction rapidly, the industrial pollution and labor exploitation have become visible, people's social and environmental sensibilities have increased and the brands have started to develop their strategies in this direction. This has reached such a level that fast fashion brands have deceived their customers by greenwashing.[6] The best way to prevent this is through brands becoming transparent about their supply chains.

Brands are able to share everything with their customers simultaneously thanks to internet and social media. Some of them have just used this opportunity to implement their transparency policies. In these posts there is much information ranging from producer names and addresses to open costs of their products which are usually considered as trade secret. Although the extent and accessibility of this information is still in brands' initiative, this new perspective accountable to the customers is very important in terms of transparent supply chains.

The Patagonia's Black Friday[7] campaign in 2011 tells in a beautiful way how a marketing strategy can be correctly used. Starting with the slogan "Don't Buy This Jacket", the company shared with the public the amount of waste, water and carbon dioxide caused by its 60% recycled polyester jacket (Patagonia Website, 2011). Therefore, it gave its customers the message that no matter how a product is eco-friendly, has long life and durability, it always has an effect on the environment.

Figure 2.3. Drawn based on the photos taken from the above-mentioned campaign by Patagonia (e.n.). Illustration: Kardelen Aysel

Practices that create social benefit such as making people who produce the products visible by including them in the stores, donating to an NGO a certain share of each product purchased as well as steps considering environmental effects like using energy-saving lamps may seem small in the beginning, however when the general influence of textile industry is considered, they have the power to create big changes.

The last link of the chain: the effect of consumers

Production and design techniques of which every step are carefully thought and a profit sharing that allows textile workers to live in better conditions are very important for slow-fashion. However, it is not possible to break this vicious circle without noticing the overconsumption that consumers are forced into. Whether all these efforts in the supply chain will be meaningful depends on the purchasing behavior of consumers who are the most important link of the chain.

Fast fashion takes its power from the poor quality garments as a result of low prices and the rapidly-changing trends that prevent their poor quality from getting noticed. The solution is to deny to be a cog in the machine, purchase less but wisely and slowdown against fast-fashion. In order to reduce our environmental and social damage, we should check our wardrobes if there is a real need before buying new clothes, borrow if possible, prefer secondhand and vintage stores or local brands rather than global ones.

The most important responsibility of the consumers is to question the clothes they buy, put pressure on brands for transparency and encourage other people to be more conscious. By acting collectively in this path, we have the power to force even the global brands to consider their environmental effects and produce ethically.

Bibliography

Chung, S.-W. (2016) Fast fashion is "drowning" the world. We need a Fashion Revolution! [Online Source] https://www.greenpeace.org/international/story/7539/fast-fashion-is-drowning-the-world-we-need-a-fashion-revolution/ [Accessed 22 April 2018]

ClimateWorks Foundation. (2018) Measuring Fashion, Environmental Impact of the Global Apparel and Footwear Industries Study. [Online Source] https://quantis- intl.com/wp-content/uploads/2018/02/measuring_fashion_report_quantis. pdf [Accessed 22 April 2018]

Crabbe, C., Wong, M. and Yanz, L. (2015) Living Wage Now! [Online Source] https://asia.floorwage.org/resources/essays-and-reports/living-wage-now-magazine/view#document/p3 [Accessed 23 April 2018]

Ditty, S. (Ed.). (2017) Waste is a Design Flaw. Loved Clothes Last, 1(2), 12. 41.

Gordon, J.F. and Hill, C. (2015) Sustainable Fashion Past, Present and Future. Oxford, Bloomsbury.

Greenpeace. (2017) Detox. [Online Source] Greenpeace.org: http://www.greenpeace.org/archive-international/en/campaigns/detox/timeline/ [Accessed 22 April 2018]

Kaur, A. (2018) Banana Fibre a Revolution in Textiles. [Online Source] http://www.fibre2fashion.com/industry-article/7654/banana-fibre-a-revolution- in-textiles [Accessed 25 May 2008]

Kerr, J.ve Landry, J. (2017) Pulse of the Fashion Industry. Global Fashion Agenda & The Boston Consulting Group. [Online Source] http://globalfashionagenda.com/wp- content/uploads/2017/05/Pulse-of-the-Fashion-Industry_2017.pdf [Accessed 22 April 2018]

Known Supply Website. (2018) Celebrating Makers. Known Supply. [Online Source] https://knownsupply.com/. [Accessed 25 June 2018]

Orange Fiber. (2018) The Idea. [Online Source] http://orangefiber.it/en/ [Accessed 25 June 2018]

Patagonia Website. (2011) Don't Buy This Jacket, Black Friday and the New York Times. Patagonia. [Online Source] https://www.patagonia.com/blog/2011/11/dont-buy-this-jacket-black-friday-and-the-new-york-times/ [Accessed 25 June 2018]

Pinatex. (2017) The Manufacturing Process. [Online Source] https://www.ananas-anam.com/ [Accessed 25 June 2018]

Hoskins, T. (2015) Rana Plaza Factory Collapse History Cities 50 Buildings. The Guardian [Online Source]

https://www.theguardian.com/cities/2015/apr/23/rana-plaza-factory-collapse-history-cities-50-buildings [Accessed 25 June 2018]

Stotz, L. and Kane, G. (2015) Global Garment Industry Factsheet. Cleanclothes. [Online Source] https://cleanclothes.org/resources/publications/factsheets/general-factsheet-garment-industry-february-2015.pdf [Accessed 22 April 2018]

Anonymous Writer (2013) The Impact of a Cotton T-Shirt. WWF [Online Source] https://www.worldwildlife.org/stories/the-impact-of-a-cotton-t-shirt [Accessed 22 April 2018]

http://supply-chain.unglobalcompact.org/site/

Notes

1   Consumption apprehension defending that environmental collapse can be prevented by simple changes in consumers' spending habits. (Kellogg, Scott; Pettigrew, Stacy; 2007)

2   Minimum charge required for covering a worker's basic needs.

3 Sustainability Apparel Coalition is a constitution embodying many textile companies, commercial unities, academic institutions and members of America Environmental Protection Agency; aiming at creating a system targeting not to cause environmental loss and a positive social effect for textile, foot wear and ready wear industries. (https://apparelcoalition.org/)

4 Higg Index is a series of measurement system consisting of a variety of tools and measuring the sustainability performance of a product or a firm in terms of environment and sociability. (https://apparelcoalition.org/the-higg-index/)

5 The Asia Floor Wage Alliance is an organisation where labor unions and labor and human rights organizations work together with the aim of providing Asian labourers with sufficient wage. (https://asia.floorwage.org/)

6 A firm's marketing their product or service as "environment-friendly" essentially not being so though. Instead of making their operations environment-friendly, such firms spend their resources on marketing campaigns which tell that they are like so.

7 Black Friday, is the first Friday comes after Thanksgiving Day in America. On this day, which is considered to be the beginning of Christmas shopping season, stores make huge discounts.

Figure 3. Slow Studio connects designer, producer and consumer (e.n.).
Design and Illustration: Kardelen Aysel

Slow+Fashion: Revisited
Hazel Clark

Introduction

This chapter revisits and updates some of the ideas and examples I shared in the article "Slow+Fashion: An Oxymoron-or a Promise for the Future...?" (2008). During the ten years which have intervened there has been a considerable number of publications on fashion and sustainability in academic journals, books, and for the general reader.[1] Yet the "slow" approach taken in my article has not been developed substantially in relation to fashion. In this chapter, I will reflect on some of the premises I proposed in 2008, and will add some updated examples, in order to question anew the value of the concept of "slow" to fashion today and going forward. The original article was inspired by a "Slow+Design" symposium which I was invited to attend by designer and theorist Ezio Manzini in Milan in 2006. That event was organized jointly by slow food specialists and design practitioners, based on the origins of slow thinking in the Slow Food movement, founded by Carlo Petrini in Italy in 1986 to preserve traditional and regional cuisine and local ecosystems. For fashion, I argued in my article that the slow approach should not be seen simply as the literal opposite of or just in reaction to fast fashion. Rather, it offered a more thoughtful and informed approach towards the "repositioning of strategies of design, production, consumption, use and reuse," which were already emerging alongside and posing potential challenges to the premises of the global fashion system (Clark, 2008: p.428).

Philosophically, Wendy Parkins and Geoffrey Craig's expanded concept of slow living proved a valuable point of departure. In their book of the same name, Parkins and Craig describe slow living as "a process whereby everyday life…is approached with care and attention [in]…an attempt to live in the present in a meaningful, sustainable, thoughtful and *pleasurable way*" (Parkins and Craig, 2006: p.ix in Clark, 2008: p.429). Subsequently, the everyday has gained more of my attention, as the basis for a new critical framework for the study of fashion and its history. This was explored in detail in the book I co-authored with Cheryl Buckley, *Fashion and Everyday Life: London and New York* (2017). In it we argue that in everyday life fashion should not just be determined by the "fashion system" and by commodity-driven processes, but also as a cultural phenomenon that facilitates embodied identity (Buckley and Clark, 2017: p.1).

The "Slow+Fashion" article likewise addressed fashion through some "evolutionary approaches, posited on new relationships between human beings, the display of their self-images and the actual clothes they wear" as models for a more socially aware design. These were potentially slow strategies that had the capacity to challenge the existing hierarchies which existed, for example, between "designer", "producer", and "consumer," amongst others. Questions were raised over fashion being concerned exclusively with the "new," by highlighting fashion's propensity to reiterate former styles, as well as to incorporate the reuse, recycling and upcycling of garments. Fashion's reliance on images was also challenged in order to acknowledge the material relationships between wearers and their clothes. From an individual's perspective fashion provides independent choice, and the tools for the expression of identity, and does not merely have to follow a market-driven mandate. Investigation of these approaches highlighted collaborative and cooperative ways of producing garments, which, in particular, provided greater agency for women. (Clark, 2008: p.429).

In order to explore these propositions, the 2008 article was organized according to the three "lines of reflection" that had served as a structure for the original Milan symposium, namely: the valuing of local resources and distributed economies, transparent production systems with less intermediation between product and consumer, sustainable and sensorial products that have a longer useful life and are more highly valued than typical "consumables." Design-based examples were provided, which drew upon cultural practices and techniques that were local to their places of origination, including Brazil, the USA, the United Kingdom and Italy. The production systems involved highlighted transparency, and the products appealed to senses other than only the visual, especially to the touch. Design innovation was key to each of these initiatives.

Returning to this topic ten years later, I have once again sought out examples of good practices that appear in different ways to be demonstrating the slow strategies, and the lines of reflection which structured my original thinking. New developments in the intervening period have enabled me to select examples of design-based initiatives that are local to my home base in New York. This re-evaluation presents the opportunity also to reflect on the discourse which has evolved, in the academy and in the public realm, since 2008. Together these enquiries bring me back to question the very state and nature of "fashion" and to advocate for a more expansive definition and understanding of the term than is often current. In seeking examples of businesses that correspond to the original "slow+fashion" tenets, I sought out initiatives which had not existed in 2008. Each offered design as a creative tool towards "slower" fashion, highlighted transparency and traceability of production (sometimes directly back to nature), questioned fashion being concerned exclusively with the new, and featured collaborative and cooperative work, especially by women. Discussed in turn below, they are: Study New York, friends of light, and Eileen Fisher RENEW.

Design

Study New York was founded in New York City in 2009 by Canadian Tara St James and highlights its principle of "Making Fashion without Making Waste" (http://study-ny.com). In common with other small scale and ethically inclined companies, its website is key to telling the brand story as a form of communication and education for consumers. It declares that Study NY utilizes Slow Fashion, which it describes as "the movement of designing, creating, and buying garments for their quality and longevity," based on "slower production schedules, fair wages, lower carbon footprints, and (ideally) zero waste" (http://study-ny.com). As part of this objective the company promotes the transparency of its supply chain, "from field to cutting table," to ensure that "every part of a garment's process is carefully examined and controlled to be socially and environmentally conscious." It cuts and sews its collections domestically using ethical fabrics and production methods, and aims to integrate clear design thinking. Its commitment to transparency for the customer is reinforced with garment labels designed to share all the details from the fiber used to the process of manufacturing.

By defining itself through conceptual design and sustainability, Study NY aims "to better the fashion industry and the world" (http://study-ny.com) while challenging preconceived ideas of fashion and design. Its mission is not merely to sell clothes, but is also one of educating consumers about what is involved in the designing and making processes. The aim is to produce well-made garments that will withstand the test of time, rather than short-lived items for a fashion season. To this end in 2013 it went "off [the fashion] calendar to create a uniform collection of eight to ten styles, in a few colorways, that is enhanced by capsule pieces" (St James, 2017). The designs utilize basic shapes, including a jumpsuit and a shirt which provide versatility and are intended to encourage creativity by wearers (Figure 3.1). As with other similar initiatives, wearers are encouraged to value individual items of clothing as having worth in their everyday lives, not based on the price tag or the fashion currency of a look or a brand.

Figure 3.1.Study New York, Shirt sleeve dress made using vintage men's shirts, part of the Uniform Collection Courtesy of Tara St James, 2016. Photograph by Sacha Maric

Another initiative with a strong ethical foundation, which similarly conforms to my three lines of reflection is friends of Light, a weaving cooperative which develops and produces jackets shaped to individual bodies. Based in the Hudson Valley in upstate New York, the cooperative takes advantage of its location to partner with small-scale fiber producers to source materials and with spinners to develop yarns. One example was Buckwheat Bridge Angoras, a wind and solar powered fiber farm and spinning mill in Elizaville, New York which provided locally spun yarn for the second prototype, part of the first iteration of an ongoing series, With Light, which was presented in November 2015. The resulting garments used a warp yarn of 70% mohair and 30% fine wool in natural colors, and a weft yarn is 20% mohair and 80% white wool blended with different percentages of colored goat fiber in black, brown and white (Figure 3.2). In common with all garments made by the collective, they were woven on purpose made back strap, and frame looms. This produces pattern pieces that have complete woven edges (selvages) and therefore do not need to be cut, but can be interlaced to construct a jacket. The design emerges from the materials and from methods developed to weave two-dimensional cloth into three-dimensional form, that might be considered a kind of "new couture" approach (Figure 3.3). Each jacket is the expression of the collective knowledge of the people involved in its creation. The selling price of the jackets reflect the amount of handwork involved in their production, but also that they are "investments" rather than "disposables," made and designed for longevity and for comfort. The cooperative is comprised mainly of women, who work together and interchangeably in a domestic setting very much in the historical traditions of female textile collectives.

From left to right; Figure 3.2. Jacket by friends of Light. Courtesy of friends of Light, 2015. Photograph by Shari Diamond Figure 3.3. Garment under construction, friends of Light Courtesy of friends of light, Photograph by Dora Somosi

The third case study is also located in the Hudson Valley, in Irvington New York, and again headed and run mainly by women. RENEW is a program run by the Eileen Fisher company, which repurposes in different ways returned garments that were bought from the company. Better quality pieces are cleaned and then sold online or at select Eileen Fisher stores. Items in good condition, but with flaws or stains, may be overdyed with natural dyes, or mended and resold in selected stores. Anything damaged beyond repair would be deconstructed and the usable parts would be formed together to create new garments. Experiments have been conducted to reuse fabric, for example by felting, as another way of repurposing discarded clothes. This process draws attention to the individual used garment, recognizing how it in effect becomes unique and gains its own "social life" once it is purchased and worn (Appadurai, 1986). Design and making skills are used to give renewed value to garments that were once discarded and designated as "rubbish" (Thompson, 1979). Through the RENEW process clothing items re-enter the commodity market, arguably with enhanced value, as original pieces rather than as part of a mass-produced series.

Each of these design-based case studies highlight slow approaches to fashion outlined in my original article and mentioned above. In particular, they draw attention to transparency and traceability, they question fashion being concerned exclusively with the new, and they feature collaborative work, especially by women. They are not underpinned by the desire for high profits, the motivation behind their design and evolution is more ethical and educational; they encourage fewer and more considered purchases, and longer and more lasting relationships between wearers and their clothes. Even the largest of the three companies, Eileen Fisher, utilizes the net profits from the sale of renewed clothes go to programs that support positive change for women, girls and the environment. In order to move ahead with slower strategies for fashion we need more ethically inclined examples of this sort and there also has to be a shift of attitude and understanding on behalf of the wearer.

From the perspective of design, production, wear and education, much of the slow innovation in fashion is being initiated and delivered by women. Perhaps this is not surprising, for historically and cross-culturally women have had a long and deep relationship to cloth and clothing. While fashion has been called capitalism's "favorite child" (Sullivan 2017) Peter Stallybrass reminds us that,

> The gendering of cloth and of attitudes to it, has itself been materially inscribed through social relations: outside the capitalist marketplace......it has been women who were both materially and ideologically associated with the making, repairing, and cleaning of clothes.
>
> (Stallybrass in Hemmings, 2012: p. 73)

It is not only in the design and production of "slower" fashion and clothing that women are making an impact today, but also in revitalizing fashion's discourse in order to add intellectual substance and a greater level of knowledge to the slow fashion conversation.

Discourse

Over twenty years ago, the late American feminist and political theorist, Iris Marion Young, commented how clothes have often served as a way to bridge differences between women. In doing so she drew upon the French feminist philosopher Luce Irigaray's proposition that patriarchal masculine desire is obsessed with identifiable objects than can be seen, but that women's desire is plural, fluid, and interested more in touch than in sight. Young comments how "feminine experience...affords many of us a tactile imagination, the simple pleasure of losing ourselves in cloth" (Young,1994: p.205). She describes the relationships women have to and through clothing and cloth, referring to the bonds of sisterhood that are formed via clothes, through the likes of shopping and sharing individual items of clothing. Young also notes how women often have stories to tell about their clothes and how connections are formed through their telling.

The relationships between women and their clothing were also explored through the ethnographies which form the basis of British anthropologist Sophie Woodward's research which resulted in *Why Women Wear What They Wear* (2007). Using the approach of "wardrobe studies" Woodward interviewed women in the presence of their clothes to investigate their attitudes about what they wore and how they dressed relative to their sense of self and identity construction. Scholar Efrat Tseelon had also previously used a wardrobe approach in her empirical studies which privileged ordinary everyday clothes, rather than extraordinary fashion items (Tseelon, 1994). While this approach is not unfamiliar amongst fashion scholars, it has helped to establish a more public discourse about clothes.

In 2014, two books were published which highlighted for general audiences the associations of women with their clothes. The first, *Women in Clothes* is attributed to its three, New York-based authors and to the "639 other" women of different ages, nationalities and occupations, who contributed a variety of stories, examples and insights to the book about their relationships with their clothes (Heti, Julavits and Shapton, 2014). In the same year artist and writer Emily Spivak published *Worn Stories*, 2014, a collection of clothing-inspired narratives based on her interviews with individuals. It was followed in 2017 by a second volume, *Worn in New York*, described as a collection of "sartorial memoirs" that linked their female and male wearers to the city. The book underlined how clothes gain emotional value when worn, and thus challenged the predominance of exchange value in fashion, predicated on high prices or fashionable brand names. In doing so it reiterated the need for a more nuanced and insightful definition of fashion, which challenges market-driven premises, and the privileging of fashion images, over the relationships of actual clothes to real bodies. According to my argument, this recognition can be facilitated by a slower and more considered approach, which can result in a much-needed re-definition of "fashion" which would encompass human as well as market values. Other scholars and writers appear to support this view.

(Re) Definition

In 2013, journalist Elizabeth Cline drew attention to the negative impacts of fast fashion in *Overdressed: The Shockingly High Cost of Cheap Fashion*. Targeted at a general reader, her book provided evidence of how the declining prices of clothes referenced poorer production conditions for workers, had served to increase consumption, and had resulted in greater material and human waste. Seeking a more optimistic future for fashion, Cline drew attention to "slower" principles, including the fact that smaller-scale production could provide more exclusivity and desirability for fashion garments. She noted how "By supporting local talent, slow clothing also has the potential to re-establish local and regional style lost over recent decades" (Cline, 2013: p. 210). Thinking strategically about a new slower fashion approach, Cline referenced British scholar Kate Fletcher's work on the "craft of use" (Fletcher, 2016). Fletcher's research resulted from her Local Wisdom project conducted in a number of cities around the world (2009-13), including New York (2013). Using ethnographic research methods, examples of re-design, and stories and images from people of how they used their clothes, the book articulated a new political agenda for fashion. It was stated as one whereby we "choose what we are and what we do with clothes daily is to have the power to alter the fashion system...tales of "material consciousness" with fashion collected from the public become tiny lessons of change" (Fletcher, 2016: p. 23).

Such evidence of changing practices reiterates the need for a re-definition of the term "fashion" to encompass slower thinking and actions, to acknowledge also fashion's material values and fundamental relationships to people. There is also a necessity for a coherent fashion discourse, which will include the work of fashion experts and those from other fields. Towards this I would offer philosopher Jane Bennett's "new materialism" (Bennett, 2011) and Jonathan Chapman's "emotionally durable design" (Chapman, 2015). Chapman's text in fact returns us to the words of Ezio Manzini who called in 2001, for the creation of "islands of slowness" that allow for re-thinking and re-evaluation about the ever-changing world (Chapman, 2015: p.83). For fashion, the three "lines of reflection", continue to offer a viable "slow" structure, as outlined above and in the three case studies. This can be achieved by: valuing local resources and distributed economies; the implementation of transparent production systems with less intermediation between product and consumer; and creating sustainable and sensorial products that have a longer useful life and are more highly valued than typical "consumables". But to be effective it will demand new attitudes to the design, production, and use of clothing. What will be required also in that process is greater reflexivity towards creative and ethical potential and collaborative agency, to enable a stronger and more considered relationship with the stuff of fashion – our clothes.

Bibliography

Appadurai, A. (ed.) (1986) *The Social Life of Things.* Cambridge- UK, Cambridge University Press.

Bennett, J. (2011) *Vibrant Matter: A Political Ecology of Things.* Durham-NC, Duke University Press.

Buckley C. and Clark, H. (2017) *Fashion and Everyday Life: London and New York.* London and New York, Bloomsbury.

Chapman, J. (2015 [2005]) *Emotionally Durable Design.* London and New York, Routledge.

Clark, H. (2008) Slow + Fashion: An Oxymoron – or a Promise for the Future...? *Fashion Theory: The Journal of Dress, Body and Culture* (Vol. 12, Issue 4). p.427-446.

De Klee, K. (2016) friends of Light: Handwoven jackets from New York [Online Source]

http://www.designindaba.com/articles/point-view/friends-light-handwoven-jackets-new-york [Accessed 28 April 2018]

Heti, S., Julavitts H., Shapton, L. & 639 others, (2014) *Women in Clothes.* New York, Penguin Group.

Parsons, W and Craig, G. (2006) *Slow Living.* Oxford and New York, erg.

Spivak, E. (2014) *Worn Stories.* New York, Princeton Architectural Press.

Spivak, E. (2017) *Worn in New York: 68 Sartorial Memoirs of the City.* New York, Abrams Image

Stallybrass, P. (2012) Worn Worlds: Clothes, Mourning and the Life of Things, in Hemmings, J. (ed) *The Textile Reader.* London and New York, Berg. pp. 68-77

Sullivan, A. (2017) "Capitalism's Favourite Child." *Socialist Review*, May (424). [Online Source]

http://socialistreview.org.uk/424/fashion-capitalisms-favourite-child [Accessed 25 April 2018]

Thompson, M. (1979) *Rubbish Theory.* Oxford, Oxford University Press.

Tseelon, E. (1995) *The Masque of Femininity: The Presentation of Women in Everyday Life.* London, Sage Publications.

Woodward, S. (2007) *Why Women Wear What They Wear.* Oxford and New York, Berg.

Young, I.M. (1994) Women Recovering Our Clothes in Benstock, S. & Ferriss, S. (eds.) *On Fashion*. New Jersey, Rutgers University Press. pp. 197-210.

Websites

https://www.eileenfisherrenew.com [Accessed 2 May 2018]

http://study-ny.com [Accessed 27 April 2018]

Interviews

Author interview with Tara St James, Study New York, September 19, 2017

Notes

1 These include, for example, but are not limited to: Brown, S. (2010) *Eco Fashion*, London: Laurence King; Gwilt, A & Rissanen, T.(2011) *Shaping sustainable fashion changing the way we make and use clothes*, London: Earthscan; Black, S. (2012) *The Sustainable Fashion Handbook*, London: Thames and Hudson; Fletcher, K. & Grose, L. (2012) *Fashion & Sustainability: Design for Change*, London: Laurence King; Ricchetti, M & Friza, M.L. (2013) *The beautiful and good: Reasons for sustainable fashion*, New York: Rizzoli; Fletcher, K. (2013) *Sustainable fashion and textiles: design journeys*, London: Taylor and Francis; Farley, J. (2014) *Sustainable fashion : past, present, and future*, London and New York: Bloomsbury Publishing; Hethorn, J & Ulasewicz, C. (2015) *Sustainable fashion: what next? A conversation about issues, practices and possibilities*, New York: Bloomsbury; Subramanian Senthilkannan Muthu (ed) (2017) *Textiles and Clothing Sustainability Sustainable Fashion and Consumption*, Berlin, Germany, Springer-Verlag.

Figure 4. Emotional connection with clothes (e.n.).
Design and Illustration: Kardelen Aysel

Locating Emotionally Durable Fashion: A Practice-Based Approach
Alex Esculapio

Introduction

In a report from 2017 by not-for-profit British organisation Wrap[1], emotional durability is understood as a concern with clothing's lasting "relevance and desirability to the consumer" (2017: p.5) and mentioned as a valid approach to design for longevity. This understanding is aligned with design theorist Jonathan Chapman's framing of emotional durability as a conceptual framework for designers to create products that encourage long-term user attachment (Chapman, 2005, 2015a). The ambition of emotionally durable design can be said to overlap with the aims of slow fashion practices, including the extension of the lifetime of garments and a considered re-thinking of the user's agency in fashion activities (Clark, 2008, Fletcher, 2010).

However, fashion researcher and scholar Kate Fletcher (2012: p. 222) has questioned whether this product-centric understanding of emotional durability is applicable in fashion, arguing instead that durability is more often than not the accidental outcome of how we use clothing and therefore largely outside of designers' control. By extension, this means that the material qualities of fashion products do not necessarily result in emotional durability.

This chapter seeks to offer a conceptual bridge for these two perspectives by proposing an approach to framing the relationship between emotional durability and fashion based on the concept of fashioning. After a brief discussion of the literature on emotionally durable fashion and on fashioning, the chapter will show how the two concepts intertwined in an installation that aimed at locating emotional durability in fashion. The display strategies will be discussed alongside the outcomes to demonstrate that emotional durability can be located across fashion practices. What emerges is a framing of emotionally durable fashion as a process rather than a set of tools and strategies.

Fashioning emotional durability

The term "emotional durability" was coined by design theorist Jonathan Chapman to describe the possibility of "a deeper and more sustainable bond between people and their material things" (Chapman, 2015b: p.79). By extension, emotionally durable design describes a set of tools and strategies to create, nurture and sustain long-term relationships between users and products. Chapman himself has suggested this framework can be applied in fashion and has proposed a definition of what emotionally durable fashion might be:

> Emotionally durable fashion is adaptable and capable of modification, it uses materials that age well and grow old gracefully, it is designed to be repaired with low levels of skill, and it avoids fleeting trend to occupy a slower and more enriching style space (Chapman, 2015b: p. 79).

This definition highlights the commonalities between emotionally durable fashion and slow fashion approaches, which may focus on "extending the lifetime of garments" through "greater attention on valuing and knowing the object … and design that generates significant experiences" (Clark, 2008: p. 439-40). The framework for emotional durability, in this sense, can provide useful tools to both understand and encourage slowness and longevity in fashion.

There are, however, two potential issues with Chapman's definition. The first is that it frames fashion as a product-centric and industry-led phenomenon, failing to acknowledge that it is first and foremost, in the words of fashion scholar Jennifer Craik, a form of "clothing behaviour" (1993: p.3) that largely relies on the symbolic value of clothing. This is particularly relevant when addressing durability and sustainability because, as Fletcher points out (2012: p.228-9), making clothing last is not the same as making long-lasting clothing: use practices, rather than industry-led innovation, largely determine the meanings and values that may result in clothing that is emotionally durable. The second issue is that the definition is based on a theoretical framework rather than on examples of existing fashion, thus framing emotionally durable fashion as a proposal for the future. But as fashion studies scholar Hazel Clark writes with regard to the applicability of slow design principles to fashion, it is desirable to "move beyond the theoretical framework to uncover not just potentialities, but what already exists" (2008: p. 429).

These reflections provided the theoretical background for the installation Beyond Ephemeral, which was included in the exhibition Imaginative Investigations at University of Brighton that took place between 27 February and 18 March 2017. More specifically, the display sought to locate emotional durability in fashion in order to expand our understanding of emotionally durable fashion beyond product-centric views and to ground the theoretical framework through examples of practice.

The central concept for the display was the idea of "fashioning". As fashion studies scholar Heike Jenss notes, the term emphasises the etymological root of the English term "fashion", which is the Latin term facere ("to do"), thus enabling a shift to an "active understanding" of fashion as "a complex cultural practice, presupposing agency" (2015: p. 7). Particularly useful for locating emotional durability in fashion is the understanding proposed by sociologists Tom Fisher and Sophie Woodward, who frame fashioning as a process that occurs "between an individual and clothes, as either maker or wearer," but also "in networks of people and garments that produce the meaning of fashion" (2014: p. 8). In this chapter, I will use the terms "process of fashioning" for intentional creative processes and "acts of fashioning" for more informal ones, the latter being informed by design historian Judy Attfield's use of "act of designing" as "something that most people do everyday when they put together a combination of clothes to wear or plan a meal" (2000: p. 17). By extension, the installation can be considered both as the tangible product of a process of fashioning and as a process which locates emotional durability in fashion across practices as a way of producing new understandings and meanings—of fashioning emotional durability, so to say.

Curating and/as locating: conceptualising beyond ephemeral

The discourse and practice of fashion curating has recently expanded and gained recognition as a form of critical practice (Clark and Vänskä, 2018). For the purposes of this essay, I understand fashion curating as a form of "material thinking" (Carter, 2004: p. 10) and "a way of producing knowledge ... while creating discourse" (Clark and Vänskä, 2018: p.2). This view overlaps with the understanding of fashioning as a process of meaning production that includes people and things. In this sense, the activity of fashion curation in general could be seen as a process of fashioning.

The process of creating the installation Beyond Ephemeral began with a consideration of the central theme of my research and of the space available for my display. The title of the display was meant to highlight the fact that emotionally durable garments and the concept of emotionally durable fashion itself challenge the notion of fashion as intrinsically ephemeral and fugitive, a narrative that goes back to late 19th century theorists of Western modernity like Charles Baudelaire and Georg Simmel (Buckley and Clark, 2012: p.18). In contrast, my research and the display focus on long-lasting garments and the emotional value users may imbue them with.

In terms of space, the exhibition occupied the communal areas of the Art School building at University of Brighton and it largely consisted in wall space. After careful consideration, I selected a wall in the foyer that offered enough space to potentially exhibit different kinds of materials, i.e. garments, images, ephemera and so on. Moreover, no mannequins or dressmaker forms were available throughout the duration of the exhibition. This greatly limited the display possibilities for clothing and, by extension, what fashion curator Jeffrey Horsley has described as "the myriad of possible contextual narratives that relate to clothing and wearer" (2014: p. 78).

Displaying only garments seemed to be the most visually impactful choice. Conceptually, this linked to Chapman's understanding of emotional durability as an outcome encouraged by objects. The process of selection also coincided with the process of locating emotional durability in fashion. In order to challenge industry-centric understandings of emotionally durable fashion, it was key to show how emotional durability could be located "on a scale ranging from extraordinary to ordinary" (Buckley and Clark 2012: p.20), from designer fashion to everyday acts of dressing. For this purpose, it was essential to include a selection of garments that included designer pieces and ordinary clothes (Figure 4.1).

Figure 4.1. Left to right: Sheepskin coat handed down by my grandfather; silk top with human hair embroidery by Anja Connor-Crabb; painted jeans from Martin Margiela's Spring/Summer 2004/5 collection; secondhand jumper with embroidery after Otto von Busch's Textile Punctum project. Photograph by Dora Souza Dias.

The installation also had to respond to the central theme of the exhibition, which was the concept of practice as research. I therefore included two items of clothing from my wardrobe on the far left and far right—to materialise my own positioning as a researcher. The display articulated the process and structure of research: while the first garment on the left materialised both my own positioning and the process through which a garment had unintentionally become emotionally durable, each of the others represented a different case study from my PhD thesis. In turn, each garment represented a different approach to understanding and locating emotional durability in fashion.

Negotiating flatness and ordinariness

The display strategies were conceived in parallel with the process of garment selection. The unavailability of mannequins and the flatness of the exhibition space informed my decision to show the garments on hangers. This decision also coincided with my desire to display these pieces as if viewers encountered them in everyday fashion spaces such as a wardrobe or a shop.

However, at a conceptual and visual level I decided to distinguish between the hand-me-down from my grandfather which had unintentionally become emotionally durable and the other designer pieces which displayed intentional design strategies. Therefore, the first was hung on a metal hook whereas the other three pieces were displayed on wooden hangers. This strategy was meant to create a subtle visual contrast between my coat, which looked like it was hanging from a rack in a non-descript mundane space, and the other garments, which were displayed following a clean aesthetic that could translate in both exhibition and commercial spaces (Figure 4. 2).

The lack of mannequins or visuals, as well as the garments' lack of specifically gendered elements, nonetheless suggested that all the items could be worn by anyone. This was meant to encourage viewers to see themselves as potential wearers, users and creators of meaning themselves—as participants in the process of fashioning.

Last but not least, paper tags were also used, one for each garment. These paper tags were specifically chosen because of their similarity to ordinary price tags in shops. Once viewers approached to read them, however, they would find out that the text on them focused on the items' emotional value rather than their monetary one. The tags provided descriptive information and some background on the designers and design strategies behind some of the garments.

Figure 4.2. Side view of installation. Photograph by Dora Souza Dias.

Locating and understanding emotional durability through garments

As mentioned above, each garment was meant to represent a case study from my doctoral research. By extension, each also showed a different approach to understanding and locating emotional durability in fashion.

The jacket on the far left (see Figures 1 and 2) was a hand-me-down from my maternal grandfather. This jacket was passed down from him to my father and from my father to me; thus, it is an example of how an ordinary garment can become emotionally durable in informal ways (Fletcher, 2012: p. 222). I wear the jacket because of its functionality—it provides warmth and comfort in the winter months—but also because of its sentimental value—it represents a connection with both my grandfather and my father. These two elements are intertwined in the feelings of warmth, shelter and safety that the materiality of the jacket provides. The jacket has become especially important after I moved abroad several years ago; its biography suggests that the act of wearing it has given me a way to connect to my family and to materialise part of my personal identity.

The second item from the left (Figure 4.3) was a piece from designer Anja Connor-Crabb's 2012 graduation collection, Past:

Present. The collection is comprised of garments in plain organic cotton and silk designed to encourage users to personalise them through different creative strategies. This premise overlaps with Chapman's idea that emotionally durable products and their meanings should be designed to change and evolve with their users (Chapman, 2005: p. 90).

The top included in Beyond Ephemeral displays one of the strategies devised by Connor-Crabb, which was inspired by Victorian mourning jewellery: human hair embroidery. The designer herself demonstrated the strategy by collecting hair from teachers and colleagues to create the decorative patterns on the shoulder details, thus memorialising the making of the collection. Connor-Crabb herself explains the process: "it was very much about embedding personal memory in a garment but also perhaps about the memories that can be made while interacting with a garment. So through your experience with the garment you then have a different relationship with it" (Connor-Crabb, 2016: n.p.). In this sense, Connor Crabb's garment shows not only that a designer can create the conditions for users to interact with clothing at a deeper, more emotional level, but also that the creation of emotional value is the result of a process of fashioning, which in this case corresponds to the act of "tinkering with clothes" (Connor-Crabb, 2016:n.p.).

According to research by Sophie Woodward, the longevity of clothing may partly rely on their ability to materialise personal memories through the act of wearing (2007: p.54-5). Her observations seem to confirm Chapman's theory that objects that are imbued with personal meaning and memories can provide rich "narrative experiences" through time and thus may become emotionally durable (Chapman, 2015: p.116). In this sense, each act of wearing this hand-me-down could also be considered as an act of fashioning that intentionally or unintentionally materialises its emotional durability.

Alex Esculapio

78

Figure 4.3. Connor-Crabb's top with human hair embroidery on shoulder details. Photograph by Dora Souza Dias.

The third garment from the left was a pair of painted jeans from Maison Martin Margiela's menswear line from 2003/2004. These represented my case study on the fashion house's painted garments and accessories from the haute couture and ready-to-wear collections from the 1990s and 2000s. As curator Kaat Debo notes, covering materials and objects with paint is a really important yet overlooked aspect of Margiela's overall work (2008: p. 9) and branding strategy. White paint in particular became synonymous with the brand itself (Maison Martin Margiela, 2008: n.p.) and was often used to give a new life to secondhand garments and accessories.

Painting was equivalent to erasing the previous history of these objects and present them as new. As a conceptual level, this process is similar to Margiela's use of recycling and upcycling.

As the jeans in Beyond Ephemeral show, the paint was meant to fade, crack and chip off through time; by simply using them, the original material underneath the paint would slowly reveal itself and show patterns of wear unique to each user. This may encourage user attachment and potentially result in emotionally durable jeans. Chapman describes regular jeans as an item that defies obsolescence: "jeans are worked on, sculpted and personified over time" (2005: p. 116). Covering them with paint highlights the future process of use, wear and tear while simultaneously directing the attention of the wearer and of onlookers to the process itself. In this sense, these jeans display a process of fashioning from the perspective of the maker—the covering of materials in paint—and an act of fashioning from the perspective of the wearer—the act of wearing.

The last garment from the left functioned as a summary of the installation in that it combined both unintentional and intentional emotional durability. This is a vintage designer piece I bought two years ago during a research trip and later got stained during a lunch at university. The garment accompanied me through doctoral studies—it was on its way to accidentally becoming emotionally durable—but I stopped wearing it because the stains would not wash out. Simultaneously I was researching designer Otto von Busch's Textile Punctum, which was part of a series of "abstract accessories" (Von Busch, 2009: n.p.). The project consisted in a kit with an essay, red thread and needle which aimed to encourage users to highlight stains by embroidering their contours. Even if the stains would eventually wash out, their memory would be kept alive by the presence of the thread. A sign of failure or distraction was transformed into a decorative element in the process.

The kit is no longer available, but it inspired me to do the same with my sweatshirt (Figure 4.4). It was a slow, meditative activity. The garment came to represent one more part of my research process, but also embodied my agency. Its value also shifted: it went from a vintage designer piece which could be resold to a potentially unsellable but cherished item. The emotional value of the piece grew to the detriment of its monetary value, but at least I would wear it again. Woodward explains how "dormant clothing" that lies unused in our wardrobes can potentially become "active" again in many ways, including alteration (2007: p. 57-8). Von Busch's project also offers a different perspective on emotional durability: it shows that narrative experience is not necessarily maintained by the material qualities of the object; rather, sometimes it can be nourished through other forms of design intervention which engage users themselves in processes of fashioning like alteration.

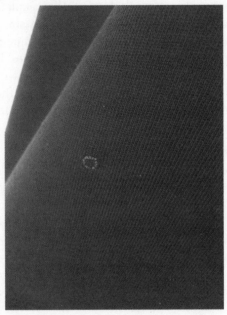

Figure 4.4. Embroidery detail on vintage sweatshirt. Photograph by Dora Souza Dias.

Conclusion

The installation Beyond Ephemeral aimed to locate emotional durability in fashion through a practice-based approach in order to propose new understandings of emotionally durable fashion. In this chapter, I analysed the selection and display strategies to show how emotional durability can be both an intentional and unintentional outcome, thus bridging Chapman's and Fletcher's perspectives, and may emerge across a range of material processes, including the design process and the myriad everyday acts that occur during the object's useful life. Therefore, I propose a definition of emotionally durable fashion as a range of processes and acts of fashioning which materialise the emotional value of clothing, thus creating the conditions for emotional attachment and potentially extending the lifespans of fashion objects. Conceptually, considering emotional durability through the lens of materiality may offer new possibilities for understanding as well as materialising slower, longer-lasting and more emotionally engaging user experiences with clothing. The installation discussed here is an example of how we could look at fashion practice, in this case fashion curation, as a process of fashioning emotional durability: the garments and display strategies highlight the people and objects involved in the material networks in which emotional durability is fashioned. In doing so, the installation also produced new discourse and meanings around the concept of emotionally durable fashion.

Acknowledgements

I would like to thank to the staff at ModeMuseum Antwerp for giving me access to their library and archives. I would also like to thank Anja Connor-Crabb for accepting to be interviewed for my PhD thesis and Dora Souza Dias for documenting the installation.

Bibliography

Attfield, J. (2000) *Wild Things: The Material Culture of Everyday Life*. Oxford and New York, Berg.

Buckley, C. and Clark, H. (2012) "Conceptualizing Fashion in Everyday Lives." *Design Issues*, 28(4). pp. 18-28. Available through: https://www.mitpressjournals.org/doi/pdf/10.1162/DESI_a_00172 [Accessed 14 March 2018]

Chapman, J. (2005) *Emotionally Durable Design: Objects, Experience and Empathy*. London and Sterling, Earthscan.

Chapman, J. (2015a) *Emotionally Durable Design: Objects, Experience and Empathy*. London and New York, Routledge.

Chapman, J. (2015b) "Prospect, seed and activate: advancing design for sustainability in fashion." Fletcher, K., and Tham, M. (eds.) *The Routledge Handbook of Sustainability in Fashion*. London and New York, Routledge. pp. 74-81.

Clark, H. (2008) "SLOW + FASHION— an Oxymoron—or a Promise for the Future...?" *Fashion Theory*, 12(4). pp.427-69446. Available through: https://www.tandfonline.com/doi/abs/10.2752/175174108X346922 [Accessed 14 March 2018]

Clark, H. and Vänskä, A. (2018) *Fashion Curating: Critical Practice in the Museum and Beyond.* London and New York, Bloomsbury.

Connor-Crabb, A. (2016) Interview with the author. 24th April 2016.

Craik, J. (1993) *The Face of Fashion: Cultural Studies in Fashion.* London and New York, Routledge.

Debo, K. (2008) "Maison Margiela '20' The Exhibition." *Maison Martin Margiela '20'* the Exhibition. Antwerp, MoMu Publishing. pp. 2-12.

Fisher, T. and Woodward, S. (2014) "Fashioning through materials: Material culture, materiality and processes of materialization." *Critical Studies in Fashion and Beauty,* 5(1), pp. 3-23. Available through: www.ingentaconnect.com/ contentone/intellect/csfb/2014/00000005/.../art00001 [Accessed 14 March 2018]

Fletcher, K. (2010) "Slow Fashion: An Invitation for Systems Change." Fashion Practice, 2(2), pp. 259-266. Available through: https://www.tandfonline.com/ doi/abs/10.2752/175693810X12774625387594

Fletcher, K. (2012) "Durability, Fashion, Sustainability: The Processes and Practices of Use." *Fashion Practice,* 4(2), pp. 221-238. Available through: https://www. tandfonline.com/doi/abs/10.2752/175693812X13403765252389 [Accessed 14 March 2018]

Horsley, J. (2014) "Re-presenting the Body in Fashion Exhibitions." *International Journal of Fashion Studies,* 1(1), pp. 75-96. Available through: www. ingentaconnect.com/content/intellect/infs/2014/00000001/00000001/ art00005 [Accessed 15 March 2018]

Jenss, H. (2015) *Fashioning Memory: Vintage Style and Youth Culture.* London and New York, Bloomsbury.

Maison Martin Margiela (March 2008) "Interview with Maison Martin Margiela: Chapter 1." *Cream Magazine,* issue 9. pp. 122-129. 70

Von Busch, O. (2009) "Textile Punctum: Embroidery of Memory." Available through:http://selfpassage.info/textilePunctum/textilePunctum.htm [Accessed 15 March 2018]

Woodward, S. (2007) *Why Women Wear What They Wear.* Oxford and New York, Berg.

Wrap UK (2017) "Sustainable clothing: A practical guide to enhancing clothing durability and quality." Available through: wrap.org.uk [Accessed 14 March 2018]

Notes

1. Wrap UK is a British charity organisation which works with the public and private sectors to implement circular economy models. It also produces independent yearly reports on sustainability in the clothing and textile sectors.

Figure 5. Co-creating through crafts (e.n.). Design and Illustration: Kardelen Aysel

The Traces Of Craft in Slow Fashion: Designer and Crafts(wo)man Collaborations

Duygu Atalay

Introduction

We can easily argue that the fashion system nowadays is on the edge of a crisis. In a paradoxical way, the enormity of the crisis originates from the extent of the system and the quick and intense flow of information that we have never experienced before. What we have lost as the flow of information increased are concepts of narrativity, storytelling and memory which the philosopher and theorist Walter Benjamin emphasizes. In modern period, while all organisation happens in an information frame, experiences are trivialized. Within this period we have focused so much on numeric and technical data that we cannot see the whole any more. Fashion is produced and used up at a great pace which is extraordinarily in a different way than the previous century and the human affairs network in the system is completely in a wrecked state. In this system in which nobody knows nobody, the designer can be from Europe, the producer can be from Africa, the consumer can be from America. It would not be wrong to define these clothes as "homeless" that have no stories, swaying from side to side, eventually easily discarded. The solution, is to suddenly turn into storytellers ourselves while we listen to the storyteller's experiences and stories. That is to say, it lays in our unity and in what we have forgotten.

In his book called *Passages* Benjamin claims that authentic works have "aura"s radiating around (2016). This radiance in works with "aura"s arises from their being "here", "now" and "unique". However, as a result of the perishment of life based on tradition in postindustrial societies, mass production, commodification of imageries and images, works with "aura"s disappear (Sevim citing from Oskay, 2010: p.511). This disengagement in works of art is in question also in clothing design. As "the concept of uniqueness" is brushed aside in order to make more production, the phenomenon of traditionality which creates it is profoundly shaken (Sevim citing from Benjamin, 2010: p. 511). Craftsmen of today become mere laborers (Sennet, 2009).

While individuality is in the foreground in design and art, in artisanal production the practice of "making together" is in the foreground because the transfer of empirical knowledge takes part at the heart of the craft. And slow fashion movement highlights the concept of collaboration by standing against this structure without "aura" created by global system. In this chapter, before scrutinizing the importance of the craft that is at the heart of fashion, how it has been excluded by global system is mentioned. By referring to new possibilities created by examples based on togetherness of the designer-craftsmen potential difficulties to be encountered have been underlined. And it is pointed out that we need a proper solution for dynamics of today instead of exactly applying the ones we knew once upon a time and forgot. Fashion itself, making us always focus on being at present and expressing the spirit of time, has been the inspiration for this.

The unwanted of global system: craft

The economic system based on global capitalism has influence both on identitites and craft products which are cultural production items. Anthropologist and structuralist Claude Levi Strauss, by saying that what creates our culture is the language, emphasizes that all indicators and symbols function like languages and mentions that tangible items too incorporate meaning in social practice (Bocock, 1992: p. 233) While the act of craft and products carry symbolic meanings within the culture they are created, the craftsman creating the item makes a cultural production when he knows what he has done and why he has done; that is, when the craftsman makes a work entirely with physical labor in an innately cognitive interpretation process. The structure that the global capitalism threatens is precisely that. For instance, in fashion system, instead of making a clothing by sewing or embroidering all pieces from beginning to end, craftsmen producing at global markets make in pieces. One person makes only the collar of the clothing, another sews pieces of sleeves and the other does the embroideries. In this way, these people are not craftsmen creating the product; but they are "laborers" created by the system and they are alienated to what they produce (Marx, 1971).

The cultural formation resulted in globalization is shortly defined as "consumption society". The aims of global companies supporting the consumption society are to market the highest number of products in the broadest geography that they could transmit in the shortest time and to do that with nondurable commodities. All people of the world are labeled as "consumers" without taking their national cultures into consideration and the result is devaluation both in the quality of products and in human affairs. In this process which is defined by sociologist and philosopher Zygmund Bauman as "new world disorder" the meaning is sought not in the process of items' production, but in consumption. Temporariness is the core of consumption and "the culture of consumption society is not related to learning but mostly forgetting" (Bauman, 2014: s. 94). Now many objects that are productions of machine are put aside despite the fact that they are not actually worn out. For consumers it is more important to buy the latest version rather than using it in the longest run (Sennett, 2009: p. 147).

The biggest problem for producers in consumption economy is that production takes time. "Goods to be consumed shouldn't require long preparatory work and, any skill to be learnt, it should provide instant satisfaction; but the satisfaction should also come to an end as soon as the time required for using up consumer goods is up. And this time should be minimized as much as possible" (Bauman, 2014: p.94). In such a system, what is expected from the craftsman is to put aside their abilities in order to enhance the production rate; in other words to forget their abilities. Because global capitalism stands against practices that are exerted with hand labor and requires quality and time. However, the skill is at the heart of craft and gaining the skill requires repetition. Today in many countries with a long-established tradition of craft like India, the intergenerational knowledge transfer have come to an extinction since embroideries which require time to be applied are considered costly (Scarce, 2003: p.452). Furthermore, this situation not only occurs merely in India but also in many Third World countries. The target to constantly introduce new and cheap products to the consumer in the fashion system cause these craft practices to be forgotten; but as Levi-Strauss cites, it also causes devaluation of items with symbolic meanings, for the consumer only appearance is made important rather than meaning.

The significance of the concepts of craft and collaboration in slow fashion movement

Slow fashion movement developing against this system which came out as a result of globalization has been emphasizing on labor intensive manufacturing, quality and craft from the very beginning. Slow Food Movement (Clark, 2008., Fletcher, 2010) pioneering this movement is a social movement started in Italy when it was realized that food culture's heartwarming nature emphasizing on unity and solidarity could be shaken by fast-food culture. According to this, a McDonalds restaurant opened in Rome is not only an ordinary fast-food restaurant; but also a blow striken against localness, traditional production, diversity, health, ecosystem, crafting, the delight taken from ingredients and the experience of unity (Fletcher, 2010: p.261). Thus, it encounters with the resistance of those who want to preserve their culture. This resistance also gives inspiration to slow fashion movement and in 2006 the manifesto of slow fashion was declared (Clark, 2008). This movement looks for solution not only in the material, but also in the culture and people producing it.

While design historian and theorist Hazel Clark (2008) defines slow fashion as giving time for production, value creation and cultivation of quality, design activist and academician Kate Fletcher (2008) advocates that the concept of fast fashion standing up against slow fashion is actually related to greediness rather than time. Either nature or producers pay the cost of every clothing bought cheap (ibid.). The way to avoid exploitation is to create structures in which producers and creators know each other and can work together instead of the global system's nature that is undermining the process of the design and production. We can observe that during its development process slow fashion movement has engaged with the concept of collaboration. Slow design processes are explicit knowledge based, collaborative, sharing-oriented, cooperative and transparent (Straussi and Fuad-Luke, 2008). Thus, they create opportunities for designs to develop and evolve into future.

Throughout the history, the phenomenon of quality in fashion has been identical with high fashion and craft. The industry of ready-made clothing developing later on, rather than promising for innovation in design, actually creates cheaply manufactured versions of creative forms and details based on hand labor that forms the essence of high fashion. And today fast fashion system carries on with following fashion shows of companies making creative designs based on labor and producing similar but simplified designs of them (Fletcher, 2010). That is to say, what is still valuable are those produced with care. Nowadays craft turns into a symbol of resistance in the face of economical and cultural changes occuring on a global scale (Scarce, 2003). This activity which is defined as "the weapon of the weak" by the anthropologist James Scott is a symbolic power increasing the commitment to local culture, family and the society (Scarce, 2003: p. 450). In recent years, a significant increase in practices based on the association of the designer and the craftsman is in question. Since the craft is an active weapon to fight against unemployment and poverty, in developing countries collaborative projects are in demand, at the same time it also constitutes an important part of design industry in developed countries like Italy, France and Spain (Richard, 2007: p.3). While these associations have the understanding of fast fashion, which has been placed and normalized by global capitalism within the last 20-30 years, and types of production questioned, it also enables new practices to spring in design culture.

New possibilities created by design practices based on associations of the designer and craftspeople

Concepts of "collaboration and co-creation" are outstanding practices of this movement. However, this is different from the logic of coproduction in conventional sense. When we analyze constitutions adopting new design practices based on the association of the designer and the craftspeople in terms of designing, producing and the way of thinking, we encounter with three significant points.

1. Development of a common language: creation of a more democratic design environment

While the practice of craft essentially based on constant repetition of the same process is in a fixed structure, design is variable and dynamic. In case of coproduction, both sides share the experience and implicit knowledge of what the other one needs but does not have. While defining the implicit knowledge contemporary philosopher of science Michael Polanyi says that "we can know more than we can tell" (1967: p.4). In case of the association of the designer-craftspeople, revealing the knowledge, which cannot be shared orally or in written way, but rather by "making together" is in question. By this means, the problem of "craftspeople becoming labourers" (Sennett, 2009) which emerged as a result of conventional system is avoided. Depreciation of the labor and the laborer is prevented. Indeed, as Clark draws attention to coproduction playing a part in the nature of craft production, she emphasizes that evoked feelings of responsibility and trust increases commitment to local culture (2008: p.434).

In the conventional system a hierarchical structure is in question within design companies. In the matter of decision making mechanism the designer and people responsible for expenditures are in the foreground. Those realizing the weaving or stitching either have a limited voice or they are voiceless about the design. In case of practices based on togetherness, the circumstance becomes different and many brands of slow fashion push the limits of creativity within the frame drawn by local craft production. In most of these examples, we witness that designers from developed countries work with craftspeople in developing countries. Although this situation is pleasing for fair share of global assets, we can think that cooperation of designers in developing countries with craftspeople again in developing countries would contribute more to the state of being good on a global scale. Thus, the stereotype of design where the center is in Europe-North America, and center of production is in Asia, Africa, South America can give way to new possibilities and slow fashion's emphasis on locality can get more response. What is pleasing is that such examples have increased in recent years.

For example, Argande, a brand from Turkey, re-customizes

weaving types and fabrics intrinsic to the region of Southeast Anatolia with local craftspeople and designers. Nearly 150 craftswomen that work with the company contemporize the cultural heritage that is centuries old as a result of the collaboration with the designer. While local fabrics are used in some designs, in others new materials are used and they are combined with the local ones (Argande, 2018) (see brand stories p. 211). Carla Fernandez, a Mexican company, also leads the association of the designer-local craftspeople in developing countries. In the mould system which they later named squareroot, they contemporize traditional square moulds used by local craftspeople that are based on folding. In the network established by the company, there are many craftspeople making handicrafts and textiles from every region of Mexico (Carla Fernandez, 2018). El Salvadorian brand Soüf also presents a good example for designers working with craftspeople in developing countries. Sofia Avila, the founder of the brand, working with nearly 20 craftspeople, manufactures unique bags made of a tree intrinsic to El Salvador. As for the jewel pieces applied in bags, she works with Carlos Rauda who is a lapidary (Soüf, 2018). We see that South America has set forth an initiative that will be an example for other developing countries in the world about supporting these associations. Cooperativashop, with the essential goal to bring designers creating designs intrinsic to Latin America, promotes brands attaching importance to "doing together" and supporting their craftspeople. Such associations are valuable in terms of supporting these brands by creating new communication channels instead of putting the burden only onto the shoulders of the designer.

Even though examples to be given here are limited, association of the designer-craftspeople is a concept adopted by many different fashion brands of the world like Voz, Yakampot, Mochi, Indigeneous. The common ground of almost all of these enterprises is that a certain part of the collection consists of pieces based on local craft and a part of it consists of modern and plain pieces. Thus, while a bridge between the traditional one and the contemporary one is laid, a design aesthetic specific to these practices emerges. This sense of aesthetics creates a new language rooted in the old, based on blending the local knowledge with the current design philosophy. With this common language, meaningful and valuable products standing apart from easily wasted products are presented to customers.

2. Transparency of supply chain and new tendencies in explanation of product contents

When companies' scale of production grows, and the rate of workers and the environment's exposure to exploitation increases, consumers' chance to be informed of this situation also decreases. Due to this, slow fashion movement draws attention to transparency and fair trade (Clark, 2008). And the association of craftspeople and the designer makes it possible to share a huge amount of information, which the conventional system hides, with consumers. And for that, going beyond the labelling system in which only product content and production site are mentioned, it develops radical, and unique communication methods. The issue of how production is made is not only on the agenda of designers working with craftspeople. Today by coming together, students, academicians, designers and producers put up a struggle in a more organized way because only by building up a new philosophy and with a collective and organized struggle, the exploitation can be avoided.

While in the past how and where the production was made was not questioned, today practices are developed towards sharing this and examples like sourcemap.com are set. While in the beginning this map was developed by design students in order to share the carbon footprint created by industrial production processes with consumers, nowadays it has become a transparent supply chain sharing platform also indicating which commmunities of craftspeople companies work with. Owing to the example of "radical transparency" it has provided, it is possible to browse all the chain and producers when clicked on the map on the site (Bonanni, 2011: p.26). While presently there are brands and companies like Vivienne Westwood, Brother Vellies, Jlew, Ethical Fashion Initiative, MIMCO in fashion section, on this platform, the number of members gradually increases. While another civil formation named Fashion Revolution makes consumers and producers question themselves with the question "Who made my clothes?", it confronts companies with the solidarity of consumer-academician-student so that producing communities would not be exploited. By publishing transparency indexes, it asks companies to clearly share their supply chains (Fashion Revolution, 2018), (See Fashion Revolution Turkey, p. 229). Increase in these examples indicates that there is a growing level of awareness.

Undoubtedly, as methods of production become more ethical, the number of brands making their processes completely pellucid will increase. On the other hand, what is significant is the increase in the number of companies making public their production processes on their own accord, not only when they are questioned because it will be the indicator that an enlightenment concerning this ethical consciousness is taking place and becoming systematic. Although their numbers are few, some designers have been developing methods peculiar to themselves. One of the examples bringing her own interpretation onto radical transparency by internalizing ethical production is Carla Fernandez (Figure 5.1). The brand has developed an approach to introduce the craftspeople in their production process to buyers through videos (http://carlafernandez. com/en). By clicking on the video icons on their webpage, customers can see how collection items especially with a high craft emphasis are produced. Sharing production through videos is utterly a modern approach because videos and social media sharings create the most powerful communication sources. Thus, recording craft practices that have been made for hundreds of years and sharing them with masses are completely compatible with the ideas of laying a bridge and the concept of storytelling that the association of the designer-craftspeople would like to emphasize. In addition, craft practices can be brought up-to-date without being confined to a certain period of time. These first examples are heralds that new sharing methods and transparency strategies will develop in the future.

Figure 5.1. Inspired from the production story of a design appeared on Carla Fernandez's website (e.n.). Design and Illustration: Kardelen Aysel.

3. Transformation of places of production into places of education

The most significant practice that associations of the designer-craftspeople have brought along is the transformation of places of production into places of education. Production made as a part of slow fashion trend focuses on small-scale design carried out at ateliers instead of big factories because as the scale gets smaller, exploitation and obscurity become less (Clark, 2008., Fletcher, 2008). And production made at ateliers offers a different design experience than that at factories. When considered in terms of global scale, it is evident that a majority of craftspeople especially in developing countries do not have academic education. Structures or cooperatives where craftspeople work jointly with designers become also places of education. An example is Voz, the company that is located in the U.S. and cooperates with Chilean craftspeople doing Mapuche weaving (Voz, 2018). Or like Carla Fernandez supporting Mexican craftspeople or Argande from Turkey. The original purpose in such examples is to stregthen craftspeople with production and while doing this to establish centers that will support their education. Thus, a new social labor model develops. In associations, there is not always a one sided flow of information running from the designer to craftspeople. There is also a flow of information from the craftspeople to the designer. In addition, other individuals who belong to the community which makes production share with other members the types of crafts which are abandoned mostly because making them takes time, and the continuity of education is provided. Types of crafts in danger of extinction due to globalization are not lost thanks to this education atmosphere and are conveyed to new generations.

Besides these examples, the issue of not confining education to the space is also on the agenda. For example, there are companies like Alabama Chanin which have opened their ateliers to the training of the local community. The founder Natalie Chanin, train local craftspeople, she also collects crafts techniques into a book or publishes online in a PDF format (Chanin, 2018) (https://alabamachanin.com/the-school-of-making). In this way, education is not confined intramurally and like a bridge it is laid from the atelier to all the world. The example of Alabama Chanin shows that although globalization has a structure threathening traditions, it can play a connecting role for people at different locations (Figure 5.2). Thus, it appears before us as an education experience intrinsic to this century and slow fashion.

Figure 5.2. The drawing that visualizes manufacturing phase of Alabama Chanin's clothes made by appliqueing old t-shirts (e.n.). Design and Illustration: Kardelen Aysel.

Potential difficulties likely to be encountered

The understanding of slow fashion based on the association of the designer-craftspeople and with democratic conditions making room for education is promising. However, there are still a few primary questions that need to be answered by those who have experienced this system. For example, how can we contact the right craftspeople for production? How can we judge that payments made to craftspeople are actually fair? How can the integration of craft into fashion system which is prone to change by nature be more sustainable? How can the consumer's awareness be raised? In fact, the question that will actually create the most radical change is related to how consumers' awareness can be raised, because when this is achieved, brands will change their production types in line with demands from the consumer. Thus, designers might take on a task like raising awareness instead of just designing a product. In that case, communication established with consumers becomes more significant than before. Radical changes are essential for communication; in this context Fernandez's sharing of production with videos as cited in this text becomes prominent in terms of the awareness it creates. Another question that needs to be answered is the issue of finding craftspeople. In recent years, platforms like Sangam, Sharing the Making, Artisans of Fashion have been formed to strengthen the association. While above-mentioned platforms usually bring together designers in developed countries with the ones in developing countries, for developing countries maybe the best craftspeople are the closest ones. The most significant problems at this point are payments and business continuity. According to the article of sociologist Timothy Scarce (2003) who reviews the situation of craft communities in Third World countries, the issue of fair wages is still a vague concept and government or company supports can only be periodical. That structuring should always contribute to social and economic goodness of local craftspeople instead of being structures that developed countries use craftspeople in developing countries for global competition. Otherwise, it is inevitable that this structure will serve for a different type of exploitation. Obviously, it is not possible to create a solution by changing only one factor creating the system. Although the change begins at one point, as long as other organs creating the organism do not operate in parallel with the same purpose, permanence and change is out of question.

Conclusion

The attempt to make the design process more ethical with slow fashion movement reminds us once again that instead of producing by competing with each other, collaboration is a more humane and sustainable method. Design practice proceeding in parallel with craft activity were conclusively separated in postindustrial period. However, preindustrial craftspeople were individuals who could take roles of designing, producing and marketing. While globalization wiped out many craft activities, it also played a discriminative role in terms of relations between the past and the future, restrained craft activities to the rural while urbanizing markets (Unesco, 2005: p.4). At this very point, designers acting like a bridge, have been undertaking the task of preventing that dissociation. Models based on the association of the designer-craftspeople are utterly rewarding in this respect due to their roles of integrating the traditional with the contemporary. Owing to these associations our way of designing changes, ateliers of production turn into places of education, production becomes transparent, a common language evolves and eventually, the phenomenon of narrativeness that we have lost is revived. What is developed during associations are not only products, but at the same time human affairs. Rumi says, "A candle loses nothing when it lights another candle". In case of the association of the craftspeople and the designer, no one loses but they carry the design into a much brighter future. Thus, they together create the opportunity for creating shining works with "aura"s which Benjamin complained about withering away. The most significant thing that remains is making this change systematic and permanent.

Bibliography

Bauman, Z. (2014) Küreselleşme. (5th ed). (A. Yılmaz, Trans.). Istanbul, Ayrıntı Yayınları.

Bocock, R. (1992) The Cultural Formations of Modern Society. [In] Hall, S. and Gieben, B. (Eds.). Formations of Modernity. Cambridge and Oxford, The Open University, p. 229-274.

Benjamin, W. (2016) Pasajlar, (Ahmet Cemal, Trans.), Istanbul, Yapı Kredi Yayınları.

[Original name: Das Passagetu-erk. Frankfurt, Suhrkamp Verlag.1982]

Bonanni, L. (2011) Sourcemap: Eco-Design, Sustainable Supply Chains, and Radical Transparency. XRDS. 17(4), p. 22-26

Clark, H. (2008) Slow+Fashion- an Oxymoron- or a Promise for the Future...?. Fashion Theory, 12(4). p. 427–446.

Fletcher, K. (2008) Sustainable Fashion and Textiles: Design Journeys. Malta, Earthscan.

Fletcher, K. (2010) Slow Fashion: An Invitation for Systems Change. Fashion Practice, 2(2), p. 259-266.

Marx, K. (1971). Capital, A Critical Analysis of Capitalist Production, Vol. 1. London, Lawrence and Wishart.

Polanyi, M. (1967) The Tacit Dimension. Michigan, Michigan University.

Richard, N. (2007) Handicrafts and Employment Generation for the Poorest Youth and Women. United Nations Educational, Scientific and Cultural Organization, Paris.

Scarce, T. J. (2003) Precarious Production: Globalisation and Artisan Labor in the Third World.Third World Quarterly. 24 (3), p. 449-461.

Sevim, B. A. (2010) Walter Benjamin'in Kavramlarıyla Kültür Endüstrisi: "Aura", "Öykü Anlatıcısı" and "Flâneur". Uluslararası Sosyal Araştırmalar Dergisi, 3 (11), p. 509-516.

Sennett, R. (2009) The Craftsman. London, Penguin Books.

Straussi, C.F., & Fuad-Luke, A. (2008) The Slow Design Principles; A new interrogative and reflexive tool for design research and practice.[Online Source] http://www.slowlab.net/CtC_SlowDesign Principle. [Accessed 20 June 2018]

UNESCO. (2005). Designers meet Artisans. New Delhi, Craft Revival Trust.

Electronic Citations

Alabama Chanin (2018). http://www.alabamachanin.com/ [Accessed 2 February 2018]

Argande (2018). http://www.argande.com/ [Accessed 10 May 2018]

Carla Fernandez (2018). http://carlafernandez.com/ [Accessed 10 May 2018]

Voz (2018). https://madebyvoz.com. [Accessed 20 June 2018]

Soüf (2018). https://souf.shop/about/ [Accessed 20 June 2018]

Fashion Revolution (2018). https://www.fashionrevolution.org [Accessed 20 June 2018]

Figure 6. Design with Memory (e.n.). Design and Illustration: Kardelen Aysel

Two Fashion Tales in South Africa: Re-use as Memory Practice

Erica de Greef

Introduction

I consider upcycling and repurposing as a "memory practice", to have a longer history in South Africa than recent interest in these sustainable practices reflects. This notion repositions the fashion-and-sustainability argument into a historical and "affective" narrative, one that considers not only the tactile, practical and material concerns of environment, society and technologies, but one that rethinks the emotive and political underpinnings of what it means to recraft, reuse and remake. In this short essay, I extend on the idea of repurposing, recrafting and reintegrating as a mnemonic, subjective and creative practice, welcoming the past into the present as an active participant, not just something that must be forgotten, discarded or erased.

Story one: memory narratives on the catwalk

Showcasing at the 19th South African Fashion Week A/W 17, design duo Oscar Ncube and Mandy Newman of Vintage Zionist, presented a raw and re-engineered, upcycled leather jacket collection[1] styled with black cotton knit tunics, dresses and t-shirts; *I DON'T REMEMBER* printed in white on a number of these. The front print also includes *IN MEMORY OF* and a thin white cross, while on the back, the print includes ALL *THINGS PAST* and *THE REBIRTH.* When asked what notions of "forgetting" the designers were referencing, they maintained they were not committing to any single trace, memory, or absence and, that their use of "tombstone references" was purposefully ironic and ambivalent.[2]

My response to this printed text takes two routes. Firstly, and in line with archivist Verne Harris' call to give space to the dynamic between remembering, forgetting and imagining in post-apartheid South Africa, and the cautionary words of then president, Nelson Mandela – that forgetting first requires some difficult remembering – I suggest that the paradox scripted into this fashion item is deeply connected to South Africa's divided and traumatic past. Harris reminds us how under apartheid the terrain of social memory was a site of struggle of "remembering against … a systematic forgetting engineered by the state" (2002: p.1). Truth (represented by personal experience) replaced historical narrative, and this informed the fundamentally, curative aspect of the Truth and Reconciliation Commission – an immense undertaking of collective, post-apartheid nation building, post-1994.[3] Memory work was deemed vital for its promise of a liberated future, and in this regard, engagements with the past were obligatory.

In museum collections of dress and fashion, memory traces become important evidence of lives lived, stored in the folds, stains and scuffs of clothing. The uncanny, absent presence of the wearer is also found in objects that are no longer worn. This is noted both in objects that have been lost, misplaced, discarded and forgotten, and in objects that are treasured and remembered, and survive in personal and public collections. Clothing "receives a human imprint, where the human trace is remembered through a crease, scent or hole" (Stallybrass, 2012: p.69). As part of the new South African Museum and Archive of the Constitution at Constitution Hill (MARCH) in Johannesburg, clothing items feature as sites of embodied remembering, particularly in relation to acts of resistance during in the apartheid era. Similarly, the Workers' Museum, also in Johannesburg, draws on the evocative and often everyday, material memories of life, of composite identities, and of forms of oppression and resistance enacted through the dressed body. As artist Ellen Sampson writes, worn clothing becomes a record of individual lived experiences,

> … [they are] covered with the marks of use. Wear is materialised in clothing in many ways, in stretching, tearing, abrading and creasing. These marks are not singular, linear or orderly; instead they overlap … the process of inscription is complex; imprints jostling together non-contemporaneously. As a garment is worn, its surface becomes a map of the actions performed within it (2017).

The re-worked leather jackets in the Vintage Zionist collections evoke their histories of wear, as scuffs, scars, smells and shapes – embodied reminders of their wearers and their makers. The designers, working with thrifted secondhand leather jackets, both deconstruct (unpick, take apart, select and rescue component parts of the jackets) and reconstruct (rethink, recombine and remake as new jackets) as a means to produce contemporary pieces deeply imbued with layers of history. The deconstruction and reconstruction of the jackets at the hands of the designers both memorialise the embodied past narratives, and "forget their details"[4], as these secondhand leather items are re-engineered and presented as new. The process of upcycling pulls the "lost time" of these jackets into a dialogue with the contemporary, and in this way, disrupts the fetish of newness and evolution in fast fashion. Time here is enfolded, repeating, and slowed down by the designers' considered repurposing and remaking practices.

My second line of thought in relation to the combination of the deconstructed jackets and the use of the text on the catwalk, follows a felt, psycho-cultural impulse – I do not remember "someone" or "something" because it was denied, or it is lost, forever gone from memory, as a kind of reflective nostalgia – a kind of ongoing longing or delayed homecoming – following artist and writer Svetlana Boym (2001: p.xviii). The rhetoric of reflective nostalgia is "about taking time out of time and grasping the fleeting present", maintains Boym (ibid.). The garments on the catwalk (as the quintessential present) carry the pain of a forgotten past in a perpetual present.

Boym however identifies two types of nostalgia; the first being reflective, and the second as a restorative nostalgia, namely a "transhistorical reconstruction" of a lost time and place (ibid.). I suggest that the nostalgic sensibility at play in the work various contemporary South African fashion designers, including of Vintage Zionist, actually sees an overlapping of Boym's two "types of nostalgia"; where the fashioned nostalgia acts as a form of collective re-occupation of the past in order to re-identify with it, so as to return it to the present as restorative nostalgia, while at the same time, as wistful gestures of the past on a t-shirt, in a dress or with a jacket, perpetually keeps the past at a distance as reflective nostalgia.

Notions of memory, forgetting, loss and healing lie at the heart of various creative endeavours in South Africa.[5] I am reminded of the work of South African photographer Santu Mofokeng, with his ongoing research project *The Black Photo Album/Look at me*: 1890-1950 (1997-ongoing).[6] Mofokeng creates and curates a contemporary archive of images, composed of photographs commissioned by black working- and middle-class families of the early twentieth century, which, he points out, portray Africans in a very different manner. By re-presenting the photographs in a contemporary framework and context, and by re-claiming the subjects' neglected stories, Mofokeng produces a kind of necessary, re-visioning of the past, challenging and disrupting the ideologically biased, yet sanctioned images, enshrined in public memory, museums and archives of an African history as tradition. Fashion reworked in the present, equally carries the potential for a re-visioning of the past, particularly with regards to notions of a lived traumatic, divided and exclusionary past.

Story two: memory acts in the museum

The catalogue card of South African Museum artefact acquired in 1994, SAM14394 (Figure 6.1) states that the "tattered and wild style [of the trousers] reflects the attitude of youths at this irresponsible stage before initiation." The trousers are one of nine pairs of trousers in the ethnographic museum's collection of almost fifteen thousands sartorial objects. The long, below-the-knee pair of khaki-coloured beaded trousers, or *ibulukwe*, are cut-off in a rough, serrated, zigzag pattern, with extensive, all-over beadwork in red, white, blue and black. Some of the beadwork is quite random; some of it trained along the garment's edges, seams and hems; and some, spells out a Xhosa first name, *MPHATHI*. In addition, some handwritten names on the back legs are in thick, uneven ink pen, with outlines in black and filled in with red ink pen (*MPHATHI, BHEQEZI and ZIBUZELE*), and some in blue ink pen (*MtANAKA, MLANDLU*). [7]

The cultural "over-writing" of embellishing with beads, and tagging with names, re-scripted the cheap, mass-produced pair of Western trousers. The khaki trousers would have served originally as part of a colonial school or workwear uniform, which through the hands of women crafters, have been re-imagined, re-making the trousers so that they speak to and about a different, African postcolonial contemporaneity and notion of ownership.

Figure 6.1. Khaki-coloured beaded trousers, Eastern Cape, South Africa: SAM 14394, front and back view. Photograph by Andrew Juries, courtesy of Andrew Juries

The identities "performed" on the garment's surface, follow a graffiti trope of tagging, with five individual names claiming a shared space, a collective experience and perhaps even a mutual ownership through this singular sartorial item. The contemporary, literal use of text and the "traditional", symbolic use of beaded patterns also set up a dialectical and provocative tension between the past and the present, between remembering and forgetting, and between tradition and modernity. This brings to mind African public intellectual Achille Mbembe's notion of the temporal entanglements of the postcolony, that "enclose multiple durées, made up of discontinuities, reversals, inertias, and swings that overlay one another, interpenetrate one another, and envelope one another" (2001: p.14).

The beaded trousers present a case of overwriting and reworking of the original object, as both material and conceptual recrafting of the garment. Their original value as a generic uniform conceptually deconstructed through the stitching, cutting and beading of the object, to fashion new, cultural identities. If the fashion object has been empowered itself "has a memory through its history and social milieu, deconstruction plays with the memory by fragmenting and reconstructing [it] into a new entity, ... a new narrative" (Kipoz, 2013: p.8). The expressive transformation, and in this case with the beaded trousers, the cultural translation of the object, plays with the objects' memory, at times as a deconstruction and revival of its inherent material memories or, as in the case above, an overwriting of the original narratives altogether. Anthropologist Karen Tranberg Hansen, in her study of "salaula" or secondhand clothing in Zambia, argues that,

> ... secondhand garments do not travel with ready-made meanings attached to them. [These are] created in the practices through which they are put to use. It is in clothing performance that meanings are lodged and constructed by [new] wearers and viewers, [where] meanings [become] the product of distinct dress practices in specific situations (2009: p.113-4).

In the recrafting of "found objects", such as ready-made Western clothing, African artists and cultural producers, have been actively re-scripting objects into new narratives over the past centuries. The chronologies of time imbued within these objects are temporarily reversed, slowed down, and consigned to new social and cultural contexts. Upcycling as a design practice, unsettles the linear narratives of time of fashion objects, as they exit and then re-enter patterns of wear.

Bridging the handcrafted and machine stitched, and the past and present, the beaded *ibulukwe* trousers remember altogether new and different histories. Art historians Sandra Klopper and Fiona Rankin-Smith describe how this hybrid "collaging of imported (European) and indigenous (African) forms of dress – of combining rural beadwork with symbols of urban leisure and sophistication, like shorts and tennis shoes – became increasingly common" as large numbers of rural men began to seek work in the mines as migrant labourers (2010: p.530). An increasingly complex sense of hybrid South African identities often played out through both individual and collective sartorial choices during the first half of the twentieth century.

I am interested in the neglect, or even disavowal of the "double storied-ness" of the various beaded trousers found not only in the South African Museum, but also in the South African Cultural History Museum collections, now both part of Iziko Museums.[8] These hybrid, beaded trousers carry double narratives in museums, namely of two lives, of two separate sets of wearers, largely of two time lines, and of two distinct yet overlapping socio-political contexts. As a fashion historian, I recognise from the cut, shape and details that some of the reworked trousers date from the early twentieth century, while others are from the mid-1980s.[9] The black formal trousers of the early twentieth century, such as SACHM 94/143 TRAD (Figure 6.2.), loosened from the moorings of an earlier life[10], re-entered circulation and participated in a second historical time. A reading of the beads used, the cotton threads in the stitching, and to some degree, the actual beadwork design on the trousers, would temporally situate these beaded pairs around the 1950s or 1960s, and even perhaps, into the 1970s as trade and access to newer, cheaper materials in some areas in the rural apartheid "homelands" was quite delayed.[11]

Figure 6.2. Black beaded trousers, Eastern Cape, South Africa: SACHM 94/143 TRAD, front and back view. Photographer by Andrew Juries, courtesy of Andrew Juries

The "double-time" and "double narratives" of objects such as these, are neither noted nor acknowledged in the records of museums, which largely identify objects of "indigenous" origin by place or "tribe", and infrequently, by period or history.[12] Not only have their histories been erased, so too were the narratives of their wearers as lives lived, loved and left behind. Fashion objects in museums (as spaces for the preservation of memories), act as sites where counter-narratives can exist, and where the complexities of embodied, personal, intimate and eccentric identities that are stored in the garment's folds are commonly denied, ignored and disavowed. Instead, the focus in museums remains largely on the fixed meaning structures of a linear and chronological fashion history. The quiet, warm, felt, happy, sad, curious and altogether encyclopedic range of emotions stored in the material folds as object memories, become powerful metaphors ready for reworking of garments in contemporary realms of design. Instead of suppressing the evidence of past lives lived, recycling, upcycling, reworking and recrafting of fashion objects in the 21st century, engages with the resonances of these past narratives in ways unanticipated, and often unexpected. The re-production of memory – via deconstruction and craft thinking – affords a re-semantifying and re-structuring (both literally and symbolically) towards re-constructing values and the conventional aesthetics of modern society (Kipoz, 2013: p.7).

Design as a memory practice

The practice of slow design, of rethinking and reframing cultural memories and histories through fashion informs the deconstructive fashion approaches of various South African designers, including Darkie,[13] Clive Rundle, and design collective, Black Coffee. The collections of contemporary designers such as these bring to mind Boym's reflective nostalgia that "dwells on diverse and ambivalent forms of longing," as nostalgia that does not shy away from modernity, and that loves details rather than sweeping symbols (2009: p.14). During the widespread xenophobic uprisings in 2008, which saw South Africans violently attacking those considered to be "outsiders",[14] design collective Black Coffee presented their collection using upcycled Mozambican textiles. The placement of a culturally significant textile at centre stage (that which was being politically scorned and socio-culturally rejected) simultaneously critiqued and disrupted the politics of colonial violence enacted on black bodies and black narratives.

These considered insertions of other cultural spaces and materials, in terms of design references, also weaves in traditional narratives (of slow time) into contemporary modernities (of fast fashion). The role of slow and sustainable design not only impacts on the aesthetics of the objects, but also contributes to expanding the scope for cross-cultural dialogue and cross-generational exchange. The potential for fashion objects to act as negotiators, facilitators and mediators positions the practice of slow fashion as a key critical player in a troubled world.

Moving beyond a purely exotic gaze of the "other", I suggest that deconstructed fashion offerings such as these by Black Coffee, seek ways to imagine or craft new afro-futurist identities not only invoking alternate African futures, but also reclaiming and rewriting the lost identities or lost perspectives that have been subverted, overlooked or denied.[15] Following cultural philosopher Walter Benjamin, "it is the tiger's leap into the past and the lost, as the topical that maps the modern" (2003: p.395). What resonates from Black Coffee's work is this trace, this resurfacing or deep channeling of energies, of cultural memories, of nostalgia that is disruptive, demanding, and actively remembered.

The practice of slow design, and in particular deconstructive fashion practices, in the global South invites us to reconsider the notion of invoking subversive forms of nostalgia that unsettle the past, and rewrite futures. Fashion as the ongoing present, is a powerful platform in which to reconsider the politics of nostalgia as design practice. The ambivalence of fashion and the socially mutable languages of design allow for critical, decolonial voices to engage both materially and conceptually in the evolution of slow fashion in the 21st century.

Bibliography

Benjamin, W. (2003) *Selected Writings Volume 4, 1938-1940*. Translated: Edmund Jephcott et. al. Eiland, H. and Jennings, M(eds). Cambridge, Belknap Press.

Boym, S. (2001) *The Future of Nostalgia*. New York, Basic Books.

Harris, V. (2002) Contesting remembering and forgetting. *Innovation*, 24: 1-8.

Hamilton, C. & Leibhammer, N. (2016) "Ethnologised Pasts and Their Archival Futures: Construing the Archive of Southern KwaZulu-Natal Pertinent to the Period before 1910". [In] Hamilton C. and Leibhammer, N. (eds) *Tribing and Untribing the Archive: Identity and the Material Record in Southern KwaZulu-Natal in the Late Independent and Colonial Period: Volume One.* Pietermaritzburg, University of KwaZulu Natal Press.

Kipoz, S. (2013) Slow Fashion Ethics: Reproduction of Memory through Deconstruction. 10th European Academy of Design Conference – Crafting the Future, Gothenberg, Sweden, 17th-19th April 2013.

Klopper, S. & Rankin-Smith, F. (2010) Migrant Workers, Production, and Fashion. [In] Eicher, J. and Ross D. (eds) *Encyclopedia of World Dress and Fashion Vol1: Africa*. London, Berg Publishers.

Kopytoff, I. (1986) The cultural biography of things: Commoditization as process. [In] Appadurai, Arjan (ed.) *The Social Life of Things: Commodities in Cultural Perspective*. Cambridge, Cambridge University Press.

Mbembe, A. (2001) *On the Postcolony*. Berkeley, Los Angeles and London, University of California Press.

Sampson, E. (2017) *Creases, Crumples, and Folds*. Retrieved: h t t p : / / w w w . fashionstudiesjournal.org/2-visual-essays-2/2017/4/2/creases-crumples-and-folds-maps-of-experience-and-manifestations-of-wear

[Accessed 10 April 2017]

Stallybrass, P. (2012) Worn Worlds: Clothes, mourning and the life of things. [In] Hemmings, J. (ed.) The Textile Reader. Oxford, Berg Publishers.

Tranberg-Hansen, K. (2009) Youth, gender, and secondhand clothing in Lusaka, Zambia. [In] Paulicelli, E. and Clark H. (eds.) *The Fabric of Cultures: Fashion, Identity, and Globalisation*. London and New York, Routledge.

Notes

1 http://www.safashionweek.co.za/category/designers/vintage-zionist/collections-vintage-zionist/?post=29227&mw=ladieswear [Accessed 28 September 2019]

2 Personal communication, email correspondence, 26-30/09/16

3 http://www.sahistory.org.za/topic/truth-and-reconciliation-commission-trc [accessed 10 October 2016]. The TRC commission was to bear witness to, record, and in some cases grant amnesty to the perpetrators of crimes relating to human rights violations, as well as reparation and rehabilitation. The process and outcomes have been both highly praised and highly critiqued.

4 There is a dual "forgetting" of detail in their design process, as firstly the specific garment details are re-rendered in new configurations and thus the original design aesthetics are lost, and secondly, the stories of the jacket's original life narrative are lost in the translation into new objects. Personal communication, email correspondence, 30 September 2016.

5 Annie E Coombes (2003) History After Apartheid: Visual Culture and Public Memory in a Democratic South Africa. London: Duke University Press.

6 www.anotherafrica.net/art-culture/what-can-these-photographs-tell-us [Accessed 20 April 2016]

7 These are all male first names of various, Xhosa-speaking clans of the Eastern Cape, South Africa.

8 Eleven previously segregated museums, including the South African Museum (SAM), the South African National Art Gallery (SANG) and the South African Cultural History Museum (SACHM) merged in 1999 to form Iziko Museums.

9   SAM14035, SAM14394 and SAM14395 are all described as "manufactured", which alludes to the cheap, mass-produced quality of school uniforms, particularly in the rural areas such as the Eastern Cape. This double storiedness entails a different act, and form of overwriting

10 A necessary act of erasure occurs in the process of secondhand clothing circulation as the donated or sold artefact has no provenance, the very opposite of museal naming practices with regard to sartorial donations and purchases.

11 Personal interview, beadwork collector and dealer Stephen Long, 23 September 2015

12 Periodisation in the ethnographic classification would be 19th century, or precolonial, and certainly not specific to a decade or a single year.

13 http://www.sl10.co.za/themba-mngomezulu-darkie-clothing/
    [Accessed 12 June 2018]

14 These attacks were largely aimed at South African neighbouring nations, including Mocambique, Botswana, Zimbabwe and further north, such as Nigeria and Malawi.

15 https://en.wikipedia.org/wiki/Afrofuturism [Accessed 11 December 2017]

Figure 7. Collaborative design and consumption (e.n.).
Design and Illustration: Kardelen Aysel

Economic Models Slowing Down Fashion: Circular and Sharing Economy

Solen Kipoz

Introduction

The fashion system that stamped its mark on the 21st century has a nontransparent cycle, in which global supply chain and design, production and consumption channels coexist in more than one country. The economic model this cycle creates sets the linear production and consumption model, which is equally speed and quantity oriented. Yet, a slow, quality oriented economic model can be created if we can convert the economy, one of the three aspects of sustainability, along with nature and human beings, into a circular, solidarist and reproductive way. Such an economic model could upgrade every phase of life cycle in a constructive and reparative way. In this chapter, I support this point of view, reviewing sustainable and slow economic models alternative to the dominant economic model, and discuss how a circular and sharing economy, which is design and innovation oriented, can transform the detrimental fashion cycle into a virtuous and healing structure.

Responsive life cycles

The life cycle of clothes involves all processes, from the initial choosing of materials in product supply chain, until the end of its useful life. Evaluation of a product's life cycle is a qualitative means of evaluating the environmental effects of different processes over this lifetime (Payne, 2011). This analysis takes a look at the life curve of the product from its cradle to grave, which includes the phases of acquisition of raw materials, production, product design, utilization and product becoming waste after utilization; it determines the effects of emissions contaminating

113

the air and the water after discharging with sources included and used in the process. (Chapman, 2010: p.3). The life cycle of a product in clothing industry begins in the design room and ends at the store (Payne, agk: p.1). This highlights the key importance of the designer's decisions on issues like material choice, cutting of clothes, choice of technology and patterns, etc. during the process. On the other hand, creating responsive life cycles requires focusing on both the product's useful life and its post-utilization story. Hazel Clark (2008) an academician opening new research windows by focusing on the possibilities for combining slowness and fashion, i.e., addresses "sustainable sensorial design", a concept originating from the designer-architect Giulio Ceppi. She speaks about the story of how a product is made from the phase of raw material to becoming the end product, and the excitement over its consumption. According to Clark, the speed metaphor created by mass-produced fast fashion products obfuscates many unethical conditions like supply of materials, production methods, working conditions, distances covered during distribution; in contrast, a slower and more sustainable approach requires being more meticulous about reaching the information of and valuation of a product (Clark, 2008: p. 440).

The value chain generated by the fashion industry which applies the conventional economy model aims at taking a fashion product or service from the idea stage to different phases of production, and meeting the demands of the ultimate consumer at every level, thus turning them into economic advantage (Mengi, 2015: p. 54). In this value chain, the final target of fashion industry within the free market economy is to create value-added products[1]. Within this framework, the design is not only a phenomenon improving life quality through the solution and aesthetics it brings, but it is also one of the most significant added values, since it increases the market price of a product. In fact, "...creating added value first of all means increasing sales and profitability, secondly decreasing production costs, thirdly overcoming grievances and complaints of consumers and finally a higher level of consumer satisfaction and a greater number of loyal consumers" (cited from Jacobs (2007) by Niinimaki 2011: p.50).

If design has such a power, can it create a different value for a slower or and more sustainable product? Design can be adjusted in order to maintain for the sustainability of value chain in the industrial system; it is possible to articulate which material will be used, by whom it will be produced, how it is to be transported to consumers, even how it will be taken care of during the usage stage, and how it will be discarded. As the design theorist Manzini suggests (1995), rather than "producing by making", in which production and consumption are connected in a linear way, the designer may adopt the culture of "making by reproducing", and therefore follow a more cyclical process in which all material transformations in the process are reclaimed. Manzini (ibid), reminds us that such a making "will create a resource for self-replicating successive cycles reparative when needed, what we start off with always gives us what we end up and should , in turn, should foretell what will be done." (p. 236).

Autarky and the principle of propertylessness: Gandhi and Thoreau

According to a pioneer of ecofeminist[2] conception, Vandana Shiva, the productivity and growth-base structure of the modern world, indicates a malfunctioning development model measured by "Gross National Product". Shiva, making a reference to ecology scientist Porrit, argues that GNP as a development criterion is dysfunctional and problematical; in a money economy, GNP measuring the total amount of goods and services produced, many of which bring no benefits for the majority, presents commodity production as primal economic effectiveness, but it does not measure the effect of expenditures on ecological destruction. This means more cash in a patriarchal order, and more commodities derived through ecological destruction, and also decrease in natural wealth that women produce, in order to sustain life (Shiva, 2014: p:44-45).[3]

In the past, communities were based on local and ancient knowledge and traditions, such as ancient India, and the foundations of slow design for sustaining life and consumption were laid as a resistance to modern world, in which science and belief systems tyrannize over nature and accordingly over women. Examples of this resistence include struggles against the witch hunt "targeting at destroying the knowing and expert women" (ibid: p.60), and also against the reductive approach of the enlightenment separating science and nature, to the approach of multiplication, speed, standardization coming along with the Industrial Revolution and the Machine Age in the 20th century in Europe. Some resistance, on the other hand, promoted economic models associated individual and social sovereignty; in 1920s Mahatma Gandhi (Von Busch, 2015: p.21) challenged the British by producing his own fabric and clothes to take a stand against the colonization of India, and adopted civil disorder, nonviolence (Ahimsa)[4] and the principle of autarky. The campaigns of Satyagraha- clinging to the truth- through which this principle came to life, were weaving traditional cotton cloths on hand looms following waves of boycotting imported cloths; another action was the salt march, which was a slow and collective civil disobedience that he started to show disapproval of the salt tax (Gros, 2017).

The march for Gandhi was at the same time an action representing slowness; in this slowness there was a reaction against mechanized civilization and rapidly increasing consumption, showing a lack of faith in blind mass production (Gandhi [1909], 1933); on the other hand, manual labor, slowness of nature and of traditional knowledge did not generate idleness and stability, but a tranquil, nurturing and feminine energy in fact, for centuries, slow walking has been particularly identified with women's actions in soil and nature (Gros, 2017: p.169). Dressed in his hand-woven dothi, seeking to be purified from all pageantry of life, Gandhi's economic principle was founded on propertylessness -aparigraha– simplification, and contentedness. His principle of self-sufficiency -swadeshi- was symbolized by the cotton cloth, handwoven with the spinning wheel he developed with traditional and local craft methods, and the social welfare principle -sarvodova- adopts the principle of producing without labor exploitation, unlike the production based on others' labor in the industrial system (Patel, 2014).

In a different approach, environmentalist and naturalist writer Thoreau, lived a Diogenes-like existence for two years alone in nature in the cottage he built near Walden Lake in the United States. He arrived at the concept of civil disobedience half a century before Gandhi. According to Thoreau, the Mexican-

American war, slavery, capitalism and exploitation of resources and people resulted from the large-scale mass production in his era. In these conditions, the system of fabrication serves the prosperity of companies by exploitation of labor, rather than benefitting all people by providing adequate clothing (Thoreau, 2015: p.39). In the economy model he suggested in this context, the value of anything or action is consider not in terms of profit, but the benefit; not with what it brings in, but what it costs in life (ibid, Gros, 2017: p.83). This brings into question a meticulous calculation of the economic cost of needs, and the time required to meet them. Concerning clothes, he says "before adding to the wardrobe a person should think of how much of a required and significant work he can carry out with his new clothes" (Thoreau, 20015: p.34). On the other hand, the difference between the profit and the benefit is that profit-making actions can also be made by someone else instead of the individual. Thoreau states that "nobody can live deeply our life instead of us", showing that, similar to Gandhi, he believes that it is impossible for actions and production, like moments of life, to be transferred to somebody else (Figure 7.1.).

Thoreau warns us of the issue that we need to work more than enough in order to gain more than what we need. According to Jose Mujica, the former president of Uruguay, who lived on an old farm and donated most of his salary to charity, "When you buy something, what you spend is not money but the time you spend to earn the money" (2015 http://www.human-themovie.org). From this point, Thoreau's cottage experiment is a paradigm of micro life; he says "three chairs are enough; the first one is for solitude, the second one for friends, the third one for those to accompany me" (Thoreau, 2015: p.159). Thus, you only need to work to earn enough for a house and furniture which are the sizes that you actually need them to be. Mujica's "principle of proportionality" coincides with Thoreau's living principle, while resisting his satisfaction with simplicity and tendency for excess.

Figure 7.1. Thoreau, building his own dwelling and Gandhi weaving his own dothi with his spinner come together on the principle of self-sufficiency (e.n.). Design and illustration by Kardelen Aysel

Economy models making to slow down

Thoreau could envisage the distinction between needs and wants, the effect of brutal capitalism on people. There is no doubt that the principle of self-sufficiency was more applicable in a period when industrialization was beginning to take effect, when inputs were more discernable and measurable than currently. Gandhi could win the fight for independence hardly in 1948 and in India local fabrics handwoven with the weaving loom he made have been distributed all over the world. However, when demands, the amount of woven fabrics and the country's population are taken into consideration, continuity of this process is no longer possible without the exploitation of the workforce. Due to the low-wage workforce in the supply chain, India is one of the preferred countries, along with Pakistan, Bangladesh and Cambodia. As well as conditions of modern slavery that textile suppliers have created in these parts, hazardous chemicals used in production process not only threaten the natural world, but also human health. So much so that, as Orsola de Castro, the designer and founder of Fashion Revolution, says "now by looking at the color of rivers we can figure out what the denim colors of that season are" (River Blue, 2017).

In global supply chain, a manufacturing company produces and distributes clothes in more than one country via many intermediaries. In the year of 1993, with free trade agreements that the United States of America was a party to[5], developed countries cleansed themselves in terms of improving environmental ethics and fairness in terms of trade. However, by dislocating textile production from developed countries to developing countries, the pollution was shifted to demographically dense countries with a problematic social justice system. For this reason, today River Thames is less polluted but it is impossible to bathe in the sacred Ganj. With such a wide network, it seems almost impossible to purify fashion and make supply chain transparent, to transform fashion into a more responsible and slower cycle, in which the dominant economic model has a linear cycle building up the product cycle from the cradle to the grave.

Circular economy: zero waste design

We can form a circular model versus the linear and dominant economy model by imitating the cycle of the nature's nourishing flow and metabolism "from the cradle-to the cradle" (Mc Donough and Braungart, 2002) in which the concept of waste is nonexistent. Thus, a circular way of thinking, that is to say, turning lines into curves, weaves connections necessary for forming more positive environmental effects and longer lives within the cycle (Hethorn and Ulasewicz citing Kaiser, 2008: p. 158). This way of thinking emphasizes a circular structure in which long life products and materials replace short-lifematerials that resulted in constant energy loss. These new materials can create successive cycles, or can remain longer within a cycle (Ellen Mac Arthur Foundation, 2013). Thus, idle resources within the cycle becoming a closed circuit, create a circular economic system by recycling and re-releasing them into circulation (Figure 7.2.). In circular economy model, the design is based on the principles of "durability" and "convertibility" (Circle Economy, 2017). With design resolutions, it is possible to create more responsive and responsible product life cycles, to extend the lifetime of clothes, for instance, by using high quality materials or adopting a timeless style. This approach, particularly by preventing formation of post consumption waste, and by creating recycling possibilities, will enable materials to be retained within the system. Historian Strasser, emphasizing a dialectical relationship between that which we give up and that

119

which we want, places the concept of waste at the center of this relationship;

> "'Waste is trash, wreck, sweepings, rubbish, that is to say, the unwanted and the thing or material not needed any more. It is identified with extravagance, excessiveness, addiction but at the same time in a decadent way, also with destruction, wastage and death. On the other hand, from one aspect, desire refers to the thing longed for and yearned, with the other aspect it refers to deprivation, need and deficiency. Hence, the relationship between these two are like the relationship between dependency and depravation."
>
> (Strasser 1992: p.6)

Strasser's thesis can be summarized as;"Persistent waste gives birth to tragic desires" (ibid.). If we remember Charles Dicken's 'Golden Dustman' character (1998: p.85) who, in fashion historian Caroline Evans' words, turned the dust into gold during Great Britain's industrial revolution, we can realize that "one's trash is another's treasure". So how does mankind, forming capital even from dust, make objects and clothes useless already before their expected life is over?

Academician Timo Rissanen, a pioneer of the zero waste design system, prioritizes production processes in fashion industry as adapting the definition of waste to fashion. He defines "fabrics not used in a ready-made cloth" as waste (2013). Rissanen's approach is instrumental to understand "preconsumption waste" occurring during production process, because most of the waste fabric at an atelier is what is left in the cutting room. This waste, also called "cut-and-sew waste" and named as fabric wastage in the industry, includes almost 15% of the fabric that is cut, according to Rissanen, only in Great Britain in pattern rooms almost every year 100.000 tons of fabric is wasted (Hethorn and Ulasewic citing from Mc Quillan (2011), 2008: p.85). There is other preconsumption waste caused by waste and unsalable clothes, consisting of drapes left over from inactive rolls of fabric, pattern trials and prototypes. A significant part of textile cuttings, which do not decay in nature for at least for 200 years, are clothes cuttings. Every year, tons of clothes buried at waste collection centers create chemical waste threatening human health, while fossil fuel emissions generated by burning waste contributes to global warming.[6]

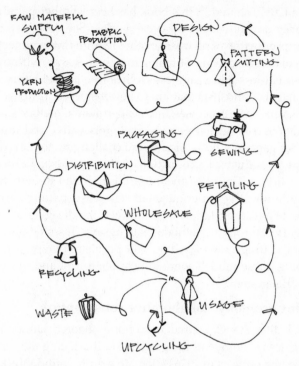

Figure 7.2. In fashion industry the circular structure in value chain will create a closed loop process in which every phase moves with curves (e.n.). Design and Illustration: Kardelen Aysel.

From the point of the consumer, as well as the physical, the emotional durability of designed clothes means consumers' do not readily discard these clothes and this makes it necessary also to think in a circular way about our relationships with our clothes. Emotional intimacy with old clothes can be reinforced by design that allows transforming, repairing, redesigning and recycling them (Circle Economy, 2017). Giving a second life to old clothes which have meanings and memories, and therefore keeping these in the cycle not only protects their memories and life experience, but it also enables them to gain new meanings with their new features. In this context, Ahimsa Collection (2012), in which new compositions were formed by the deliberate and careful disassembly of heirloom clothes, while giving them a second life created an open ended circular process in which one person was the user, designer and producer of clothes (Kipoz, 2013). Asteya

Collection (2017) shared in this book has been another paradigm of circularity as a no waste, up-cycle model. (See design stories, p.183) The production of no waste clothes requires interconnecting processes of design, cutting, stitching in a circular way; within this scope, also cut-less and seam-less clothes (see Yuksel Sahin and Sedef Acar, p.187 and 181) that are to be considered as upcycling can create zero waste processes. Such experimental methods, with both academic commercial aspects create innovative and unique designs, but generally these models are challenging to reproduce and adapt to industrial production processes. Also, European designers such as Timo Rissanen, Mark Lui, Julian Roberts have carried out innovative experiments of zero waste pattern system, which create circular relationships between the designer and the pattern cutter through methods like Jigsaw, Tessellation, and Subtraction cutting. However, due to the problems of reproduction and grading, these models were impossible to test and utilize in the industrial system.

Sharing economy: collaborative consumption

Architect Walter Stahel, a circular economy theoretician, defined "performance economy" as the principle of marketing the service rather than the product in 1976 (Ellen Mc Arthur Foundation). For example, renting and exchanging clothes make it possible to keep the source inside during the usage phase, before a new product enters into the cycle and the former one becomes waste. Instead of the conventional consumption model, such relations suggest collaborative consumption (Botsman and Rogers, 2011) practice and sharing economy defined (Zamani, Sandin and Peter citing from Belk, 2017) as coordination of gaining a source in exchange for price and distributing it. Consumption of fashion can be made circular by services enabling for renting, borrowing, exchanging in order to prevent it from becoming waste after consumption, and prolonging its life cycle. For example, in terms of environmental effects, "libraries of clothes" from where clothes can be rented in return for a certain fees or monthly subscription can reduce the need to constantly buy new clothes. On the other hand, rental clothes will create a situation close to the environmental effects created by the new ones because, when clothes change hands very often , the consumer would need to wash the clothes at least once when they rent them and once they return them, also and packaging and posting are very frequent. (Zamani, Sandin and Peter, 2017).

Clothing rental services become a way of marketing for some clothing companies aiming to reduce the environmental and social impact of product life cycles. Mud Jeans, changing buttons of the old pants and customizing them with the name of the new owner, encourage collaborative consumption, posing the question "Do you have to be the owner of the pants you wear?" Thus, by replacing "throwaway" with "use-give back" and "rent" with "buy" within the product's life cycle beginning with a circular design, it transforms the cycle into a closed circuit. The brand has also set up a packaging system named "REPACK" that can be used 20 times and can be reused by the renting consumer, annual or monthly subscription, avoiding package waste (https://7mudjeans. eu). In the denim industry, one of the most polluting textile and fashion industries in terms of water used and chemical waste released, the possibility of adopting such a consumption model is high when the used product is considered to have a durable and timeless character.

"Dress for Success", founded by young entreprenuer Nancy Lublin in 1997, is a nonprofit business model enabling women of limited income to rent suits with potential to make a good impression at job interviews. This entity presently active in 100 cities in 8 countries offers an admittedly small contribution to addressing the inequality modern society has created, but its environmental effect is significant both from its aspect of social responsibility, and in terms of promoting the circular movement of clothes (Kenny, 2012: p. 40). If we remember Thoreau's principle of utility, such as suit may cost a month's salary for a dress whose sole purpose was to impress at a job interview.

Another paradigm of the principle of propertylessness in fashion consumption is exchange activities growingly in demand in recent years. Exchange, creating a circular consumption model in terms of the consumer's giving away clothes in their wardrobe at the same time creates a social sharing platform with micro activities, bringing people together over similar world views and values. Exchange, becoming a clothing consumption model for the past decade particularly in Europe, also with the formation of "Clothing Swap" in Turkey, aims at making people care about objects "usage value" rather than "material value" by enabling the sharing of unused clothes, raising awareness of responsible consumption (see brand stories, p. 221).

Designing by sharing: collaborative design

Sharing economy can be created through design with models of "collaborative design" or "open-source design". As emphasized by the design reasearcher Hirscher and the design theoretician Fuad Luke (2013):

> "Sharing of time, gifts, talent and knowledge has begun to go beyond money with "static" (Jackson, 2009) or "descending" (Latouche 2011) "alternative economies" becoming a current issue particularly with global economic crisis. Thus, design is not a one-sided activity only professional designers design for consumers, it has become a collaborative and open-ended activity designers design together with other designers and amateurs."

(Hirscher and Fuad-Luke 2013: p.177).

For participants, such a production usually carried out at workshops at the designer's request means becoming skillful at designing and producing new clothes and in time by adopting the practice of do-it-yourself (DIY), turning passive consumers into makers, with their own voice within the system. As for designers, receiving feedback through collaboration with users enables creating social sharings that lead to the discovery of the different potentials of the design. As well as making new clothing, the act of collaborative or participant design, but sometimes can be taken by focusing on transformation of old clothes, and upcycling them through design. For instance, sessions of making together at workshops can be organized for various groups of people such as teenagers, children andproductive women who are not designers. These groups can engage in constructive activities by which they transform a piece of clothing they like, but prefer not to wear in its current state due to reasons such as size, changes in fashion, and its physical condition.

The craft at these workshops, where participants use manual labor, becomes instrumental for collaborative design strategy.This not only strengthens the production's social and solidarist aspect and subsidiary role of the craft considering design, but also breaks down gender-oriented prejudices associated with the craft (Kipoz, 2018: p.180)

Production with the craft also creates a cause for slowing down in society, if we think that "you can consume at a speed you can produce" (Flecther and Grose, 2012: p.149). An increasing number of young designers are being paid for such workshops in return for knowledge and skills. Since with such activities it is admittedly quite challenging to encourage fashion devoted consumers to reproduce instead of buying, participants usually consist of only the most responsive consumers. Therefore, it seems that the possibility of this production going beyond collaborative design activities, creating sharing economy and becoming an economic model slowing down fashion can be ensured only in the long-run (Hirscher and Fuad-Luke citing from Botsman and Rogers (2011), 2013: p.177). Alternative economy models creating a responsive and responsible design-production and consumption cycle are not able to have a fundamental impact the speed of fashion activities; but by putting fashion's dominant cycle under scrutiny, it suggests a constructive economy model in which every phase is accountable to the other, and the amount of incoming-outcoming is balanced and, possibly, decreased in proportion to needs. In the first two decades of the millennium, in which we are on the brink of economic crisis and reaching a point of over-consumption of natural resources, the value of a slow economy based on repairing, healing and recycling, may be in the hope it provides for the future rather that is current effectiveness.

Acknowledgement

I would like to express my thanks to Design Professor Özlem Er who has contributed to the development of the scientific and structural content by reading this text.

Notes

1   Added-value shaped with the addition of actual cost of the product (material, the effort spent, transferred resources) onto sale price can be considered as intermediate consumption expenditures of people and companies getting involved in producing this product. When intermediate consumption expenditures made previously by other people or companies in order to produce this is deducted from the price of goods exposed for sale, the

remaining is the odds. https://www.iktisatsozlugu.com/nedir-279-katma-deger-#.W2mXiCgzaUk

2   Ecofeminism is a thought developed against the humane domination of all components of nature like animals, earth, water, air, etc. and over disadvantaged people like women, children, the poor, the black etc. in the society (See: Warren, K (2000) Ecofeminist Philosophy: A Western Perspective on What It Is and Why It Matters. New York and Oxford, Rowman&Littlefield). It refuses reductive approach making a distinction between nature and science as well as gender discrimination.

3   If we give ear to Shiva, a constructive and ecological development model will be possible only with regaining the feminine element. In India symbolized as incarnation of the feminine element, that is to say the primary energy nature-Prakriti, the essence of everything and surrounding everything, is again nourished from its feminine side so as to procreate and maintain life (Shiva, 2014: p. 87).

4   The principle of Ahimsa which Gandhi adopted during civil disobedience acts, that is to say, showing resistance with the power of soul, not with violence and physical power -because rejecting violence embarasses violence.

5   Particularly North American Free Trade Agreement signed by Bill Clinton (NAFTA).

6   Denim manufacturing is an extremely polluting industry in terms of consumption and pollution of natural resources and harms of poisonous chemicals on nature and human health. Denim made of cotton fabric ravening for water, particularly while turning into pants consumes high amounts of water in order to derive different surface effects and to have a distressed appearance (a pair of denim pants consume nearly 3600 litres of water) and generates toxic materials. While many phases like stamping and staining cause generation of heavy metals like cadmium, chromium, mercury, lead and copper, potassium permaganate and azo colorant chemicals endanger biological life of human and natural environment (greenpeace.org and fashionrevolution.org).

7. Only in the UK, annually 2,5 to 2,7 million tons of textile consumption occurs; 1.1 to 1.4 million tons of this are clothes (WRAP (Waste and Resources Action Programme) 2013).

Figure 8. Cronological time and kairological time in fashion (e.n.).
Design and Illustration: Kardelen Aysel

Speed as Distance over Time: Reframing Fast and Slow Fashion in Australia

Alice Payne

Introduction

Fast fashion and slow fashion are critical concepts in the discussion of sustainability in fashion. In academic circles each concept has been widely studied, and in fashion media and communication, slow fashion is often set up as a contrasting paradigm to the dominant model of fast fashion. This chapter looks beyond the common definitions of "fast fashion" and "slow fashion" to instead bring the concept of fashion's speed back to first principles. As sociologist John Tomlinson (2007) observes, in physics, speed equals distance over time. What, then, are the ethical considerations for fashion in the concept of distance, and in the context of time? Through examining the spatial and temporal dimensions of speed in fashion, this chapter identifies relationships between speed/distance, and speed/time that can further inform conceptions of sustainable fashion. These ideas are discussed through analysis of the Australian fashion industry. The chapter argues that through setting aside the inevitable binary of fast fashion and slow fashion, and instead discussing speed as an ethics of distance and time, producers and consumers may come to a more nuanced understanding of what kinds of practices may contribute to a sustainable fashion system in Australia.

Beyond a binary of fast fashion and slow fashion

Fast fashion is defined as an approach to bring on-trend fashion product to market quickly through supply chain innovations such as just-in-time and quick response (Barnes and Greenwood, 2006). Fast fashion is characterized by multinational retailers such as Zara, H&M and Topshop who can bring new products into store within several weeks (Ferdows, Lewis and Machua, 2004; Cachon and Swinney, 2011). The low cost, hedonic model of fast fashion has been credited with environmental impacts such as a rise in waste and use of non-renewable synthetic fibers, as well as negative social impacts borne from increased pressures on vulnerable workers in globalized supply chains (Fletcher, 2008; Joy et al, 2012).

Slow fashion is harder to define than fast fashion, as marketing scholars Štefko and Steffek (2018) note. Slowness, as a concept, stems from the Slow Food and *CittàSlow* movement of the 1980s and 1990s and can be viewed as a reaction to the present "culture of immediacy" (Tomlinson, 2007:p. 4). Design researcher Hazel Clark (2008: p.429) identifies slowness in fashion as the valuing of local, the fostering of closer connections between producers and consumers, and the creation of "sustainable and sensorial products". Fletcher (2008: p.173), one of the first scholars to apply the ideas from the Slow Food movement to fashion, contends that "slow is not the opposite of fast – there is no dualism – it is simply a different approach in which designers, buyers, retailers and communities are more aware of the impacts of products on workers, communities and ecosystems". In practice, however, slow and fast fashion are often pitched against one another in popular and academic communication. For example, marketing researchers Joy and Peña (2016: p.37) set up an opposition of fast and slow in expressing the need for the industry to "create consumer desire for limited consumption of high-quality slow fashion as opposed to frequent consumption of low-quality fast fashion". Findings from fashion business scholars Pookulangara and Shephard (2013: p. 204) saw participants define slow fashion as "'opposite to fast fashion'; 'slowing down of the fashion product life cycle'; 'slow moving fashion styles'". The speed of fashion change was another factor: "the common theme was that it [slow fashion] is fashion that never goes out of style and is made with care and precision" (Pookulangara and Shephard 2013: p.204). Despite the obvious link with "slow" to a reduced speed of fashion change, Fletcher (2007) points out that "slow fashion is not time-based but quality-based". Presley and Meade, researchers in supply chain management (2018) concur, noting that given slow fashion is not related to speed, but rather to other qualities such as local and ethically-made, the term slow fashion may in fact be a misnomer.

Increasingly, slow fashion and fast fashion have become terms laden with value judgements. In the popular press, and indeed in academic literature, slow fashion is often used interchangeably with the terms ethical or sustainable fashion. Contrastingly, the term fast fashion has become synonymous with exploitative production and wasteful, unethical consumption (see, for example, films such as *The True Cost*). Few multinational retailers who are cited as examples of fast fashion refer to themselves using this term. A site search of Zara, H&M, and Uniqlo websites finds no mention of the term "fast fashion" in any of the brands' reports or marketing collateral. The lack of retailer identification with the term fast fashion suggests the term has become a pejorative. A fast fashion retailer is named as such by others; rather, brands themselves wish to market an image of offering "apparel of... simplicity, quality and longevity" (Uniqlo, 2018), or "fashion and quality at the best price in a sustainable way" (H&M 2018). In contrast to the negative associations of fast fashion, the term slow fashion has been eagerly grasped by fashion marketers to describe a grab bag of practices that be may loosely described as "not fast fashion", such as offering classic styles, garments handmade by artisans rather than anonymous factory workers, independently designed and manufactured locally, as well as consumer practices such as shopping secondhand and repairing one's clothing. Given this fraught use of terminology, and the increasingly solidifying divide along ethical lines in which fast fashion equates to "bad", and slow fashion equates to "good", how may we understand an ethics of speed in fashion, beyond these loaded terms? The following section examines speed as time over distance.

Speed as distance over time

The two Greek words for time, *chronos*, meaning measured time, and kairos, meaning the opportune time, illustrate conceptions of time as both qualitative and quantitative (Gault 1993). Chronos is the quantitative time of clocks and calendars, while kairos is the qualitative "right time", the moment to seize. In relation to fashion time, von Busch (2009) proposes that "fashion", meaning immaterial trends, operates in kairological time, whereas clothing, as material object, operates in chronological time. Of course, fashion production inevitably engages with both forms of time; as political scientist known for his research on politics of time Glezos (2012: p.40) puts it, "The Kairos of newness is always extended in the Chronos of history". However, the short-term trendiness of a garment, i.e. its newness to the wearer and its "fitness" for the kairos of the fashion moment, is not necessarily locked to a fixed, chronological point in time. Referring back to the original meaning of kairos, the opportune time, the right time, or a god's time, kairos may be interpreted beyond the short-term fashion fad "of the moment" to simply, "the right time" for this garment. The opportune time for a garment may come and go, and then come back again.

An ethics of time in fashion is closely related to notions of durability. Durability, as Fletcher (2008) describes, is how long a garment will last both materially and symbolically for the wearer. For a fashion garment, its "symbolic durability" may include the trendiness of the garment, namely how fashionable it is, at a given point in time, to a given wearer. This I term "aesthetic durability", and may be viewed as a spectrum from faddish to classic garment styles. Necessarily, a garment's durability both materially and symbolically must be "fit for purpose" given some items move slowly through one's wardrobe, some quickly (Fletcher and Tham, 2004). Durability can therefore be described as comprising material durability, aesthetic durability, and, following industrial design researcher Jonathan Chapman (2010), emotional durability, in how connected a wearer is to their garment. For garments to which an individual is attached, the opportune moment of that garment – its kairos – is ever-present.

I turn now to the other component of speed, distance. An ethics of distance in fashion is related to the degree of transparency or opacity in the production of a garment. It may also relate, quantitatively, to carbon miles and the distance travelled by a garment in production processes. In the slow fashion movement, as in Slow Food, "local" is a challenge to the anonymity and opacity of globalized, distant production processes. However, closeness between designers and manufacturers need not mean a literal, geographical closeness. Rather, distance can be overcome through connection and care, with traceability and the related concept of transparency a means to demonstrate the ethics of manufacture. These ideas of time as a spectrum of durability to disposability, and distance as a spectrum of transparency to opacity, will now be discussed in relation to the Australian fashion industry.

Context of the Australian fashion industry

Australia is a wealthy, post-industrial country with a small population. Its large land mass means distance matters in Australia: the major cities are hundreds of kilometres apart from one another. In the 1980s Australia was one of the first Western countries to reduce tariffs on imported clothing, taking advantage of the low-cost clothing production available in Asia (Webber and Weller, 2001). These policies had the effect of dramatically reducing the country's manufacturing capabilities in the textile, clothing and footwear industries, and the local fashion industry transitioned from manufacturing to brand management (Weller, 2007). In 2016/17, Australian clothing retail revenue was AUD\$20.3 billion, with 11,310 businesses ranging from independent retailers to chain stores (Magner, 2017). Approximately 90% of clothing is manufactured offshore and imported, while local manufacturing capabilities continue to decline (Craik, 2015). Alongside, multinational and national fast fashion retail chains have flourished since 2011, when the first overseas fast fashion retailers arrived in Australia. Eleven fast fashion retailers operate in Australia, including Cotton On, H&M, Zara and Uniqlo, with combined 2017/18 revenue of AUD\$1.8 billion (Munro-Smith, 2018).

Australia has a small but engaged community of independent brands, retailers, bloggers, charities and activists furthering the cause of socially and environmentally responsible fashion. The Australian Ethical Fashion Reports, released annually since 2013, rank brands and retailers according to their reported supply chain transparency (Nimbalker et al, 2018). Non-governmental organisations such as Oxfam and Fashion Revolution have been active in Australia, and peak industry body the Australian Fashion Council has placed support behind ethical and sustainable production. For the companies that do manufacture garments locally, the organization Ethical Clothing Australia (ECA) conducts audits on manufacturing facilities to ensure compliance with labor laws. A consumer-facing swing tag informs the buyer if the brand has received ECA accreditation. These various initiatives, coupled with television shows such as *War on Waste* (ABC, 2017), and the book *Wardrobe Crisis: How We Went from Sunday Best to Fast Fashion* (Press, 2017) have brought to the general public's attention the problems of treatment of workers in fashion supply chains, and environmental issues surrounding plastic pollution and the growing volume of textile waste.

Time and distance in Australian fashion

In this section I examine the relationships between distance, time and speed in Australian fashion. A model for understanding these different relationships between time, distance and speed in fashion can be described in two axes forming the four categories of near/short, near/long, far/short, and far/long (Figure 8.1). The axis of near to far relates to the physical distance travelled in production processes as well as the degree of supply chain transparency, for which responsibility lies chiefly with fashion retailers. Short to long relates to the length of time a garment is in use, i.e. the relative durability or disposability of the garment in time, responsibility for which lies chiefly with consumers' purchase choices and care and disposal practices.

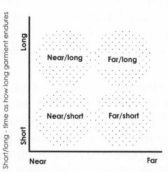

Figure 8.1. Speed as distance over time, with distance axis of near/far and time axis as short/long. Diagram: Alice Payne

An example of near/short is Cue Clothing Co., one of the few brands still manufacturing in Australia and certified by local industry body Ethical Clothing Australia. Through manufacturing garments locally (although textiles are imported), Cue is able to respond quickly to fashion trends and put new product into store within three weeks, offering up to 40 new styles in store per week (Mitchell, 2017). The price point sits in a premium mass-market level, higher than fast fashion retailers and less than ready-to-wear designer brands. Ambiguously, and relating to conceptions of both fast and slow fashion, in Cue's case, "locally-made" is a strategy to achieve supply chain speed as well as a means to support local, ethical manufacture (Figure 8.2).

Figure 8.2. Cue clothing store, Brisbane, August 2018. Photograph: Alice Payne

Cotton On, a major Australian fast fashion retailer, can be viewed as both far/short and far/long. In terms of physical distance travelled, its products are manufactured exclusively far from the site of purchase. However, in terms of supply chain transparency, the 2018 Ethical Fashion Report (Nimbalker et al, 2018) gave Cotton On an A ranking, again highlighting the ambiguity that may surround the discussion of the merits of fast fashion and slow fashion. The report authors acknowledged this ambiguity, highlighting that despite concerns regarding low-cost disposable fashion, in fact "fast fashion giants [are] doing more than most to address exploitation" (Nimbalker, 2018). Like many low-priced fashion retailers, Cotton On does not exclusively sell short term, trendy items (i.e. aesthetically disposable), but also a wide range of basic garments that are aesthetically durable for a long time. In terms of material durability, although discount fast fashion is often dismissed as being low quality, in fact, the garments have to pass strict quality control. Cost is a far more likely predicator of whether these garments will endure: regardless of the degree of material durability or aesthetic durability, the low cost of Cotton On garments and those of other discount retailers may mean the consumer is more likely to view the garment as disposable (Figure 8.3).

Figure 8.3. Cotton On store, Brisbane, August 2018. Photographs: Alice Payne

Examples of near/long Australian fashion can be found in two brands that align well with a conventional view of slow fashion. Nobody Denim, based in Melbourne, and NICO Underwear, based in Brisbane, each are small independent labels, manufacturing garments in Australia, using some Australian-milled fabric, and accredited by Ethical Clothing Australia. Each produces items that are materially and aesthetically durable, i.e. styles that are not faddish, and can thus be wardrobe staples for a long time: in Nobody's case, denim jeans, in NICO, classic, minimalist underwear.

Turning to an example of far/long, many fashion retailers in Australia cater to the portion of the market uninterested in the short-term changing trends of fashion. Discount retailers such as Rivers manufacture aesthetically stable, durable garments in offshore facilities. The brands' relationship to time in terms of aesthetic and material durability is notable, meaning stylistically they are designed to last a long time. However, in the case of Rivers, far also means opaque, with limited sustainability reporting in evidence (Nimbalker et al, 2018). Returning to the notions of distance as a meaningful, engaged connection with one's manufacturers, many independent Australian labels choose to manufacture geographically far, but personally connected. Examples of far/long include Outland Denim, a brand that owns its own Cambodian factory and received A+ for transparency in the Ethical Fashion Report, and Sinerji, a brand with close connections to communities of cotton growers, dyers and machinists in Thailand. In addition to developing these close connections to manufacturers, both Sinerji and Outland operate well outside of fashion calendars with new styles released at a slower pace.

Discussion and conclusion

The examples above highlight ways in which the dimensions of durability and transparency can be considered to avoid the easy binary of fast fashion versus slow fashion. For example, many fast fashion retailers do not exclusively sell trendy products, i.e. "short" products. Rather they sell staples such as jeans, sweatpants, t-shirts that turn over at slower speeds, are not as tightly bound to fashion trends and so may be in use for longer. Regardless of a garment's degree of aesthetic durability or disposability, given the low price point of discount retailers, it is likely that garments of both Cotton On (i.e. fast fashion) and Rivers (i.e. not fast fashion) are less valued by consumers than a more expensive item would be, and hence the garments' disposability may be increased for this reason alone. Australian fashion-forward retailers such as Cue operate on a near/short model, in that the garments are produced locally to achieve speed to market in response to fashion trends. Yet despite this speed with its implied aesthetic disposability, Cue's consumers, willing to pay the garment's high price point based on Cue's premium branding and expecting correspondingly high quality, may either retain the garments for many years, or the garments will hold excellent re-sale value in the secondhand market. In their chronological time, yes, these garments fit a fleeting fashion trend pinned to the measured time of fashion's production calendars (e.g. the trends of Spring/ Summer 2019, or first posted on Instagram on 18 December 2018), but in kairological time, these garments will materially last and continue to circulate in the secondhand market or remain in the back of one's wardrobe, until the kairos – the opportune time – is ripe for them to return.

Turning to the concept of distance, this is an area in which a multinational retailer can exercise greater demand-pull on the supply chain to ensure ethical treatment of workers and environmental issues are addressed. Unsurprisingly, in the Ethical Fashion Report, it is the large multinationals, whether fast fashion retailers or sportswear brands, who demonstrate the most rigour in ethical supply chain management. Small independents that have fostered intimate connections with their suppliers and thus have high traceability also fare well in this respect. Quantitatively, local production has advantages in reducing carbon miles, and qualitatively, in supporting local jobs and communities. However, far production is not only measured in distance travelled, but in the degree of interpersonal connection between design and manufacturing, an important point noted by Clark (2008). Independent fashion labels manufacturing offshore, may maintain strong and meaningful connections to their suppliers and their suppliers' communities, regardless of the span of physical distance.

Despite the thoughtful analysis of Fletcher (2008, 2010) in shaping the notion of slow fashion as qualitatively different from the dominant model of fast fashion, inevitably, fast and slow fashion are pitched in opposition to one another. The model described in this chapter has been an attempt to break the binary of "fast fashion" and "slow fashion" through reconsidering the meaning of speed as comprising different dimensions of time and distance. Within this model, producers and consumers each have roles to play in how an ethics of time, distance and speed in fashion may be negotiated.

Bibliography

ABC. (2017)War on Waste. [Online] Available from: http://www.abc.net.au/tv/programs/war-on-waste/. [Accessed 1 July 2018]

Barnes, L. and Gaynor L-G. (2006) Fast-fashioning the supply chain: shaping the research agenda. *Journal of Fashion Marketing and Management* 10 (3), pp. 259 - 271.

Cachon, G.P. and Swinney, R. (2011) The Value of Fast Fashion: Quick Response, Enhanced Design, and Strategic Consumer Behavior. *Management Science 57*

(4), pp. 778-795.

Chapman, J. (2010) Subject / object relationships and emotionally durable design. [İn] Cooper, T. (ed.) *Longer lasting products: alternatives to the throwaway society*. . Farnham, UK and Burlington, USA, Gower, pp. 61-76

Clark, H.(2008) SLOW + FASHION - an Oxymoron - or a Promise for the Future...?. Fashion Theory 12 (4), pp. 427-446.

Craik, J. (2015) Challenges for Australian fashion. *Journal of Fashion Marketing and Management*, 19/1.[Online] Available from: https://doi.org/10.1108/JFMM-03-2014-0017,pp. 56-68,

Ferdows, K., Michael A. L and Jose A.D. M. (2004) Rapid Fire Fulfillment. *Harvard Business Review* 82 (11), pp. 104 - 110.

Fletcher, K. (2007) *Slow fashion. The Ecologist.* [Online] Available from: https://theecologist.org/2007/jun/01/slow-fashion [Accessed 1 July 2018]

Fletcher, K. (2008) *Sustainable fashion and textiles: design journeys.* London, Earthscan.

Fletcher, K. (2010) Slow Fashion: An Invitation for Systems Change. *Fashion Practice: The Journal of Design & Creative Process* 2 (2), pp. 259-266.

Fletcher, K. and Mathilda T. (2004) Lifetimes [Online] Avaliable from: http://www.katefletcher.com/lifetimes/index.html.[Accessed 13 July 2011]

Gault, R. (1995) In and out of time. *Environmental Values*, pp. 149-166.

Glezos, S.(2012) *The Politics of Speed: Capitalism, the state and war in an accelerating world*. Abingdon, Oxon. and New York, Routledge.

Nimbalker, G., Mawson, J., Harris, C.Rynan, M. Sanders, L., Hart, C. and Shove. M. (2018) The 2018 Ethical Fashion Report: *The Truth Behind the Barcode*.Baptist World Aid Australia. [Online] Available from: https://baptistworldaid.org.au/?download_file=184252&order=wc_order_5b62ae5d58656&email=paynealice%40hotmail.com&key=73f70b47209684dd9a4d46122678c58 [Accessed 30 June 2017]

Nimbalker, G. (2018) Giving an A to Fast Fashion.[Online] Available from: https://baptistworldaid.org.au/2018/05/07/giving-an-a-to-fast-fashion/

H&M. 2018. *About H&M* [Online].Available from: https://about.hm.com/en/brands/hm.html. [Accessed 1 July 2018]

Joy, A., Sherry, J., Venkatesh, A., Wang, J. and Chan, R. (2012) Fast Fashion, Sustainability, and the Ethical Appeal of Luxury Brands. *Fashion Theory*, 16(3). Available from: doi:10.2752/175174112X13340749707123. pp. 273–295.

Joy, A. and Peñai C. (2017) Sustainability and the Fashion Industry: Conceptualizing Nature and Traceability. [In] Henninger, C.E., Alevizou, P.J., Goworek, H. and Ryding ,D.(eds.) *Sustainability in Fashion: A Cradle to Upcycle Approach*. New York, Palgrave Macmillan US., pp. 31-54

Magner, L. (2017) *IBISWorld Industry Report G4251: Clothing Retailing in Australia*. IBISWorld. [Online] Available from: http://clients1.ibisworld.com.au.ezp01.library.qut.edu.au/reports/au/industry/default.aspx?entid=407 [Accessed 26 July 2018]

Mitchell, S. (2016) Cue Clothing Co sharpens its act. Australian Financial Review, [Online] Available from :https://www.afr.com/business/retail/cue-clothing-co-sharpens-its-act-20160505-goniug [Accessed 1 July 2018]

Munro-Smith, H. (2018) *IBISWorld Industry Report OD4172*: Fast Fashion in Australia. IBISWorld.[Online] Available from: http://clients1.ibisworld.com.au.ezp01.library.qut.edu.au/reports/au/industry/default.aspx?entid=4172 [Accessed 26 July 2018]

Pookulangara, S. and Shephard, A. (2012) Slow fashion movement: Understanding consumer perceptions—An exploratory study. *Journal of Retailing and Consumer Services.*Available from: doi:10.1016/j.jretconser.2012.12.002

Presley, A.and Meade, L. (2018) The Business Case for Sustainability: An Application to Slow Fashion Supply Chains. *Engineering Management Review*, IEEE, 46(2). Available from: doi:10.1109/EMR.2018.2835458138–150

Press, C.(2016) *Wardrobe crisis: how we went from Sunday best to fast fashion*. Carlton, VIC: Nero, Schwartz Publishing Pty Ltd brand

Sanders, C.(2016): How I Learned to Stand Up to Fast Fashion. *Catalogue*. [Online] Available from: https://www.cataloguemagazine.com.au/feature/how-i-learned-to-stand-up-to-fast-fashion [Accessed 1 July 2018]

Štefko, R. and Steffek. V.(2018). Key Issues in Slow Fashion: Current Challenges and Future Perspectives. *Sustainability*, 10(7), 2270. Available from: doi:10.3390/su10072270

Tomlinson, J. (2007): T*he Culture of Speed: The Coming of Immediacy*. Thousand Oaks, CA, SAGE.

Uniqlo. (2018) About us. [Online] Available from: https://www.uniqlo.com/us/en/company/about-uniqlo-us.html. [Accessed 1 July 2018]

Von Busch, O. (2009) *Becoming fashion-able : hacktivism and engaged fashion design*. (Edited pocket version.). Gothenburg, Camino.

Webber, M. and Weller. S. (2001) *Refashioning the ragtrade: internationalising Australia's textiles clothing and footwear industries*. Sydney, University of New South Wales Press.

Weller, S. (2007) *Retailing, Clothing and Textiles Production in Australia, Working Paper No. 29*. Melbourne: Centre for Strategic Economic Studies Victoria University. Available from: http://www.cfses.com/documents/wp29.pdf. [Accessed 2 February 2011].

Figure 9. Sustainability through education (e.n.).
Design & Illustration: Kardelen Aysel

Approaches on Sustainability and Slow Fashion in Fashion Design Education

Yüksel Şahin and Sanem Odabaşı

Introduction

Impacts of fast fashion on environmental problems have been proven by scientific researches, upon adverse events encountered it has been observed that those endeavoring in the field of textile and fashion design have attracted attention to concepts like "sustainability", "slow fashion", "green fashion", and "green textiles". "Fashion" which perpetuates its existence depending on consumption has made multifaceted progresses in terms of design process and education.

Idiosyncratic cycle of fashion system activating multifaceted components has caused the birth of an enormous economy. In this cycle, the element of "design" has been located on a dominant position, the education of design has gained importance. Slow fashion, associated with sustainability, is taught at institutions which conduct design education as a course subject or within courses. Again within this content, scientific activities and researches have begun to be conducted in Turkey. The slogan of 1st International Antalya Fashion and Textile Design Biennial which took place in Antalya in 2012 was specified as "green textiles, slow fashion". Within the scope of the biennial, approaches from art and science scholars on the issue have been presented (Şahin, 2013: p.2). In addition, the project called "Sustainability in Textile Practice: Intercultural Dialogues with Traditional Symbols in Contemporary Design" conducted by The Department of Textile and Fashion Design at Mimar Sinan University Faculty of Fine Arts have revealed with epitomes how design products can be realized under the conditions of local ateliers and producers.[1] An increase in the number and quality of academic publications regarding the issue has been observed. One of these publications, the collective book called *Sürdürülebilir Moda* (Sustainable Fashion) (2015) has made the issue reach a wider audience. In the book edited by Solen Kipoz, ethical and humane aspects of slow fashion are mentioned and examples from studies made with the aim of building a new fashion system against the present fashion system are given.

Türkmen (2012: p.60), having prepared her dissertation in Turkey about sustainable fashion and textiles, become one of the leading academicians concerning this issue, mentions that slow fashion means high quality products which are carefully designed and produced, and points out that it carries the meaning for environment as less industrial waste and less discards of clothing- which means no longer to be used. As for fashion academician and theoretician Hazel Clark, in her article called "Slow+Fashion" (2008), she argues whether coexistence of fashion and slowness is an oxymoron or a new suggestion to argue against fast fashion. Indeed, in the rapid cycle of fashion new suggestions are made to become old and shelf life of products are usually a few weeks. This aspect of fashion, as also pointed out by Stuart Walker who have studies on sustainable design, contradicts with the concept of slow fashion and runs counter to the understanding with long continued processes, focusing on products with long life and being ecological (2006: p.71).

Moreover, it is understood that the focus of textile-fashion industry based on competition and sales, differs the concerns of designers in this issue. How can a fashion designer exist within slow fashion in the current paradigm of fast fashion? With unique and special designs reflecting their own point of view in terms of design, materials, content and production processes, is it possible for slow fashion to hold onto a rapidly-moving, fast pace system? As a design theoretician, Fuad-Luke asks (Strauss and Fuad-Luke, 2008: p.2), can slow design be a design paradigm to create a positive behavioral change? In reply to these questions, Clark indicates that there is an increase in the number of fashion designers wishing to be associated with slow fashion and conducting their acts in this direction; according to her this is a positive evolvement. Clark emphasized that the most challenging thing in this period is the issue of how to spread the concept of "slow fashion" to larger masses (2008: p.444).

Three researches on sustainability and slow fashion education

Within the context of our issue, it seems very difficult for a designer studying in the field of textile and fashion design to approach the subject with enough comprehension without receiving sustainability education. According to a common sustainability understanding shared by the university and the industry, realization of change is possible with sharing the knowledge (Williams, 2016: p.221). It is essential that opportunities probable to come out with transferring the knowledge and experiences to be spread within the process of education (Figure 9.1). Nurturing of honest, sensitive, compassionate designers with an eco-pluralistic understanding that Fuad-Luke mentions in his work (2002: p.15) will be only possible through education.

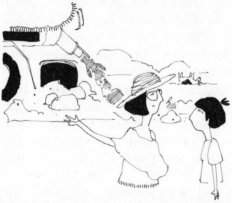

Figure 9.1. Sustainability awareness in the education of fashion design can begin with observing the environmental effects of producing fashion clothes (e.n.) Design and illustration: Kardelen Aysel

We have set forth to do a series of studies with the thought that educationisimportant for the concepts of sustainability, sustainable design, slow fashion and slow design to be understood by designers in terms of scope, content, and extent. What kept us busy the most has been the issue of how aforesaid concepts have been discussed at institutions teaching Textile and Fashion Design at university level and what kind of research studies have been conducted. As a first step, through the internet we have searched curriculums and syllabuses at undergraduate and graduate levels from websites of universities known both in Turkey and abroad.[2]

We have retained from the research that courses on sustainability are rather held at postgraduate level or the concept has been studied as a part of research projects.

The first research has been done within the graduate thesis called "The Role of Fashion Designer in Sustainable Fashion Cycle" by Odabaşı (2016). This thesis aimed at revealing how insights towards sustainability and fashion phenomena are perceived through activities of the fashion designer and what the fashion designer's role would be in the cycle of sustainable fashion. In this context, seven academicians working at departments of Textile and Fashion Design identified in Turkey have been interviewed.[3] In order to determine observations and suggestions relating to the subject, open-ended questions have been asked to seven academicians from Turkey whose are conducting projects,giving lectures and having studies on sustainability.[4] As a result of these interviews, the finding come out to be essential that to raise awareness towards fast and slow fashion, concepts related to sustainability such as recycling, slow fashion, slow design, eco-agriculture production, environmental pollution, energy consumption, discard and waste products needs to be conveyed to students with projects. Thus, the fashion designer will be able to develop solutions with their approaches towards sustainability and will have a part in the change of paradigm by serving as a bridge between fashion and textile industry and sustainability (Odabaşı, 2016: p.81).

The education part of sustainability articulated additionally on the issues of economy, ecology and equality, and named as "Education of Sustainability" at UNESCO World Sustainable Development Summit held in Johannesburg (United Nations, 2002: p.60-61). Within this context, the second research is the project called "A Study on Sustainable Development in Fashion Design: Approaches on Sustainability in Fashion Design Education and Its Contributions to Fashion Designers" that indicates the studies of the relation between sustainability in design education and the designer which are tackled in different countries to scrutinize the sort of approaches and how these take shape during the process of education.[5] Within the scope of this project schools to be researched was chosen by researching their education programs via the internet. Within the scope of the project's limits and resources, studies have been carried out including Gazi University Faculty of Art and Design Department of Fashion Design, Mimar Sinan Fine Arts University Faculty of Fine Arts Department of Textile and Fashion Design, Dokuz Eylül University Faculty of Fine Arts Department of Textile and Fashion Design, Det Kongelige Danske Kunstakademis Skoler for Arkitektur Design og Konservering (KADK) Department of Fashion Design from Denmark, California College of Arts (CCA) Department of Fashion Design, University of Leeds Department of Design. Interviews with department chairs, lecturers and students have been held and due to the organizational structures of the given institutions, issues such as sustainability in fashion design, approaches towards sustainability in the education of fashion design and the approaches of the designer to sustainability have been studied. Conclusions of the project can be summarized as below:

Academicians have found a common ground concerning the requirement of change of the current system of fashion. Realization of slow fashion with better materials, with processes of design- production and consumption have come out as a requirement in many ways. The fact that students being well-informed individuals who are concerned about emotions and senses, creating the present's design, but at the same time asking the right questions and making critiques will be possible only with a versatile education to be delivered in the issue of sustainability has been appeared among the conclusions of the project.

Discussions on slow fashion education

The study analyzing these researches conducted in terms of slow fashion has been carried out within this book as the third research. Opinions of academicians who have studies and teach on this subject have been asked in order to understand the place of slow fashion in education, to present their points of view on slow fashion, and slow design.[6] Among the people whose opinions we asked are Prof. Dr. Lynda Grose, who contributed to literature and gives lectures on sustainability at California College of Arts, Assoc. Prof. Leyla Yıldırım from the Department of Textile and Fashion Design at Dokuz Eylül University, Assoc. Prof. Dr. Solen Kipoz from the Department of Fashion and Textile Design at

Izmir University of Economics, Prof. Dr. Stuart Walker who is conducting studies on Design for Sustainability at University of Lancaster, Prof. Dr. Kate Fletcher who carries out studies as as a researcherat Sustainable Fashion Centre as part of University of Arts London and contributed toliterature with her studies, and Dr. Mark Sumner who gives lectures in the field of Sustainability, Retailing and Fashion at University of Leeds, School of Design. The questions below were asked to the academicians:

1. Is slow fashion an answer for sustainable fashion? What is the place of slow fashion in sustainable fashion design?

2. What should be the place of slow fashion in fashion design education? (a. In terms of curriculum, b. In terms of design philosophy)

Names sorted by the date they were interviewed provided the answers below:

Lynda Grose

1. Slow fashion is often described as something that will last for a long time, and is made from good materials and robust stitching. But this isn't enough unless it's paired with use (Kate Fletcher talks about this in her book *Craft of Use*). Studies show that garments are disposed of long before the end of their useful life and if a physically durable item ends up in a landfill or natural environment, it becomes a liability, not an asset.

2. Education should avoid a binary comparison where slow is considered good and fast is bad. For example a bag that is leased to someone and then another and another person, this slows the flow of materials used to make the bag through the fashion system, but delivers a fast satisfaction of desire for the wearer. Slow and fast can coexist to good effect for the environment.

I bring Local Wisdom into the curriculum by asking students to bring in an item they have kept for a long time or has meaning to them .This exercise is from Kate Fletcher again. They quickly come to realize that fashion is much more than producing and selling clothing, much more than shopping. It's in these conversations where the nuances of fast and slow can be unpacked and reflected upon. In studio, exploring items that can evolve over time compels students to think about fiber and appropriate use in the garment and use and wear by the wearer (Figure 9.2).

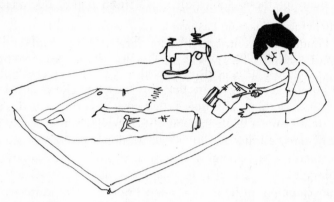

Figure 9.2. Sustainable thought transformation that design students acquire by education comes out in the way of transformation of designs of clothes. (e.n.) Design and illustration: Kardelen Aysel

Leyla Yıldırım

1. Slow fashion alone does not seem to be an answer for sustainable fashion. In a circumstance which opinions do not change on planet, universe and humans, generating new concepts only means serving to the continuity of fashion. Along with this, growing awareness on this issue has made it necessity for designers to take into account many factors besides aesthetic criteria.

2. There can be a theoretical course about the evaluation of the concept of sustainability in terms of textile, fashion and the designer or a practice-based course including a product-oriented planning. For example, a practice-based course for fashion the understanding of "zero waste" can be applied and in the textile design production processes can be questioned.

Stuart Walker

1. In my understanding, fast fashion is about producing, marketing, consuming and, relatively quickly, discarding low quality clothes that do not last; effectively, the term refers to disposable clothing. This kind of clothing is often produced by low paid workers who frequently have to put up with appalling employment conditions - long hours, abusive practices,

poor environments. This is exploitative, wasteful and anti-environmental - especially when one takes into account the fact that many of these clothes are made from non-biodegradable synthetics.

Slow fashion then, is about good materials, non-exploitative practices that enable fulfilling work, and producing clothes of quality that last. This is all very well - nice to have, one might say - but this generally means that only the relatively wealthy can afford such clothing. This does little for social equity, which is an important element of sustainability. So there is a dilemma here. Clearly, then, a transition to "slow" clothing has to encompass more than simply changing the work practices and quality of clothing. It has to also include a variety of other factors, such as: the development of new values and priorities that address our moral and environmental responsibilities, and a de-emphasis on "the latest fashions", which tends to promote dissatisfaction and psychological product/clothing obsolescence, even if the goods are still perfectly functional. This, of course, goes against the predominant neoliberal, laissez-faire economic model that has created globalized, barrier-free trade - a model that also allows environmental and ethical/human rights regulations to be easily flouted...

In addition, we can also consider what we mean by "slow". If fast fashion means overly rapid change and disposal, what does slow actually mean? If we are talking about "slow", rather than "static", we are accepting of the idea that things do change. The question, then, is one of pace - the pace of change. What is an appropriate "pace" of change? We need change not only because things do wear out, but also because we develop new ideas and can improve our thinking, our practices and our products over time. Here, then, arises the notion of "improvement over time". So we can ask ourselves, what criteria should we use to determine "improvement". Today, improvement is usually determined simply in terms of monetary profits but in the future improvement could be determined using a broader set of issues - improved environmental impact, improved labor conditions, improved shipping, reduced packaging, improved longevity, and so on. Change is inevitable. It can also be desirable. With the right values and priorities, change can be regarded as a force for the good.

2. In terms of curriculum, while there might be (a) specific module(s) on some of the history and theory of the issues, these ideas should be embedded in all courses, especially design studio courses. There should be an explicit ethical dimension to design education - because there is always an ethical dimension to design. Design is not just about facts, it involves values - but often these values are not made explicit or discussed, justified or challenged (Figure 9.3.). And in terms of design philosophy, the philosophy is about how we should live, how to live a good life that is considerate of others and caring of the natural environment, which is our home. How do we lead a good life? The notion of 'good' here is about ethics; what is right, what is wrong, what is virtuous, what is maligned. Contemporary society has placed great emphasis on individualism and self-enhancement values. Modern consumer culture fosters self-regarding values, personal status, and a preoccupation with trivial differences. We need a bigger aspiration, one that transcends self; we need to encourage "bigger-than-self" values, we need to concern ourselves with the plight of other people, other species and nature itself.

Figure 9.3. Also as young consumers, fashion design students producing critical designs that are off the influence of temporary fashion trends is also a part of sustainable cycle (e.n.). Design and Illustration: Kardelen Aysel

Kate Fletcher

1. It is one approach that works to seek to create a sector that is shaped by a positive engagement with sustainability values.

2. I see slow culture as a profound critique of consumerist society and the globalizing, commodifying mechanisms employed within fashion. Lift the lid on these structural questions within the curriculum and questions of justice, power, solidarity, fairness, justice etc. come to the fore. The curriculum then becomes an exercise in designing a new system of fashion as well as new pieces.

Mark Sumner

1. We first have to define what we mean by sustainable fashion. At a broad level this is about environment and society. But it also includes economic sustainability. It must also include reference to individuals and their physical and emotional well-being. At practical levels we are talking about greenhouse gases, water use and contamination, chemical use, discrimination, pay and working conditions, biodiversity, animal welfare, non-renewable material use, waste, child labor, deforestation, soil health, the list is endless. The suggestion that slow fashion is better and meeting all these needs is questionable and has not been proven. Furthermore, as mentioned above, the challenge that fashion is a cultural and societal process must be taken into account. Slow fashion in an abstract ideal could address some of the sustainability issues. But slow fashion in a practical reality that takes into account consumer behavior suggests that this solution is not a universal solution for all cultures, societies, groups, organizations (brands, retailers, suppliers), or individuals.

2. Slow Fashion is one of a number of approaches that can be taken to frame the fashion process, and the interaction between consumer, brand and the wider culture and society. Should it receive greater emphasis and be considered more important than any other fashion approach is questionable. Considering the role of fashion (in relation and in comparison to other aspects of fashion) and in helping consumers identify themselves in their group and society, the ability of fashion in communicating aspirations of identity and self and the ability for fashion to be

a significant source of business benefit, suggests that talking about slow fashion is valuable. To teach slow fashion as being the universal solution to the problems that fashion faces would be misleading for students and also devaluing the very important alternatives to slow fashion. As I mentioned, slow fashion has a role in design philosophy, but to argue it is more important than any other aspect of design practice is like saying high street fashion is more important that luxury, or fast fashion is more important for design concepts than couture. This is especially true when we can identify aspects of slow fashion that are no more sustainable than fast fashion approaches.

Solen Kipoz

1. First of all, for the sustainability of fashion, the system needs to repair its abrasive effects on human and nature along with itself. Within this scope, while sustainability is a more embracing concept, slowness appears as an attitude, an idea, a form of manufacturing and consumption making a way for sustainability. The relationship of design, production and consumption needs to become transparent as the word of slowness prioritizes this. The system of production and consumption created by global supply chain causes problems of unfair working conditions, cheap workforce, environmental effects increasing carbon footprint, unrepairable waste; and this creates a structure based on a linear consumption economy. On the other hand, slowness in fashion can be a marker of a circular economic structure that requires a product to be produced with care, respecting environmental, local, social and cultural resources and to be durable and long-lasting so that it would not be given off as waste.

2. A design student is primarily a consumer. Within this scope, environmental and social awareness need to be built with knowledge. A sense of responsibility needs to be conveyed in a way that the relation students have with their clothes would also form the act of design. In terms of curriculum with an approach based on transparency among the designer-producer- consumer, sustainable/slow fashion can be included in fashion design education as a course or as a program, or the character of design studios can be built in this way. Three significant elements for this will be lecturers' awareness and consciousness, research questions

of projects and giving form of feedbacks and the critical system at studios in accordance with sustainable/ethical/ slow values.

Creating a process starting with awareness and consciousness by adding social, ecological, cultural, environmental and ethical problems which need to be solved and handled in front of students; directing students in a way that they can discover design methods - recycling/upcycling, participant/collaborative design, design with craft etc.- that can be related to sustainability and slowness and find a solution in the context of research questions are suggested. In design journey, students will internalize methods in question to the extent that they can touch things and see that they can change them. Building of design approaches in a way to combine ethics and aesthetics will bring slowness and fashion together.

Conclusion

When the issue of slow fashion is considered to be closely associated with concepts mentioned above such as environmental pollution, energy consumption, eco-agriculture production, waste and discarded products, it is understood that it does not involve a narrow-scoped field. Our studies make us think that knowledge and skills that need to be acquired in the context of education for designer candidates, have to involve a broader point of view in issues of fashion's all production-consumption processes, environmental factors the world faces and the forms of manufacturing. Our survey data supports this opinion of us.

Our findings make us think that in the education of fashion design, an interdisciplinary study needs to be carried out along. In this sense, in terms of the education of the designer, studies in the scope of slow fashion should be structured together with different disciplines. The slow state of fashion and its place in the system should be discussed with other possibilities. Due to this, it is considered that the education to be given on slow fashion should not be left at a theoretical level. It is suggested that for designer candidates to consider cause-effect relations in all processes of the design to find solutions as answers to potential problems and to lay out a new business plan would be obtained by a sustainable design education.This suggestion includes doing applications so that students can understand the subject and change conventional production methods and the way of thinking. In addition, these new questions should be asked and answers should be sought through researcher's eyes so that subjects of "sustainability", "sustainable fashion", and "slow fashion" can be understood better in design education. In this sense, slow fashion itself can be questioned, discussed, facilities and limitations that it brings can be evaluated. As fast fashion has determinants, slow fashion also has certain determinants. For example, to which consumer, to which designer and for what purpose slow fashion addresses needs to be discussed. This issue can be made possible by developing a critical viewpoint in order to comprehend structures of power within the fashion mechanism. The issue of sustainability should not be associated with only slowness. It is possible to state that when it is only focused on slowness, other components are overlooked.

According to these research findings, we have carried out the education components; the issue of "slow fashion" is different from the issue of "sustainability" but it has been identified as an important field within its subject. This importance takes its source from the close relationship fashion system has with production-consumption. While the concept of sustainability refers to an extensive and new philosophical dialectic for life, can "slow fashion" be an alternative for clothing requirements that industrial forms of life are in need of? Can "slow fashion" be considered as an opportunity for sustainable fashion? These issues including slow fashion itself should be discussed. In design education, not only should concepts of "slow fashion", "sustainability" be evaluated with craft making but at the same time within new textile materials and design possibilities. Thus, those carrying out studies on slow fashion can update themselves and their knowledge. They can provide an opportunity for sustainable applications in the issue of slow fashion.

Bibliography

Clark, H. (2008) SLOW+FASHION: an Oxymoron—or a Promise for the Future...?. *Fashion Theory,* Vol. 12, Issue 4, p. 427-446.

Fuad-Luke, A. (2002) *The Eco-Design Handbook,* London, Thames&Hudson.

Kipoz, S. (2015) *Sürdürülebilir Moda,* İstanbul: Yeni İnsan Yayınevi.

Odabaşı, S. (2016) Sürdürülebilir Moda Döngüsünde Moda Tasarımcısının Rolü,

Unpublished Master Thesis. Eskişehir, Anadolu University Institute of Sciences.

Strauss, C., & Fuad-Luke, A. (2008) The slow design principles: A new interrogative and reflexive tool for design research and practice. Changing the Change Proceedings. Torino, Allemandi Conference Press.

Şahin, Y. (2013) Neden 1.Uluslararası Antalya Moda ve Tekstil Tasarımı Bienali?. Akdeniz Sanat Dergisi, Ed. 7, Vol. 4, p. 1-4.

Türkmen, N. (2012) Sürdürülebilir Bir Tekstil Endüstrisi İçin "Yavaşlık" ve Alternatif Üretim Modelleri. Akdeniz Sanat Dergisi, Ed. 8, 5, p. 59-61.

United Nations (2002). Report of the United Nations Conference on Sustainable Development. New York,United Nations Headquarters.

Walker, S. (2006) Sustainable by Design. UK, Earthscan.

Williams, D. (2016). Transition to transformation in fashion education for sustainability.[In] Filho, W. L. and Brandli, L.(eds). Engaging Stakeholders in Education for Sustainable Development at University Level. Hamburg, Springer. p. 217-332

Notes

1   Turkish name of the project is translated as "Sustainability in Textile Application: Cross-cultural Dialogues with Traditional Symbols in Contemporary Design"

2   Universities under research: Dokuz Eylül University, Mimar Sinan Fine Arts University, Marmara University, İzmir University of Economics, Gazi University, Yeditepe University, ESMOD Berlin, University of Arts London, Det Kongelige Danske Kunstakademis Skoler for Arkitektur Design og Konservering, California College of Arts, University of Leeds, Universita Iuav di Venezia, Lancaster University, Designskolen Kolding, India National Institute of Fashion Technology, Parsons The New School for Design, Aalto University.

3   Thesis advisor is Assoc. Prof. Dr. Yuksel Sahin, the co-author of this work.

4   Since names met with during thesis study are codified, names are not included in this work either. Project Number:1603E129, Project Executive: Assoc. Prof. Dr. Yuksel Sahin, Project Researcher: Res Asst. Sanem Odabaşı (It is supported by Anatolian University Scientific Research Commission). This study has been carried out by making explanations about the issue to people by interviewing them on the internet and directing predetermined questions to them. Sorted out by date Lynda Grose 16.02.2018, Leyla Yıldırım 23.02.2018, Stuart Walker 09.02.2018, Kate Fletcher 08.03.2018, Mark Summer 14.03.2018 and Sölen Kipoz, 03.07.2018 were interviewed. Local Wisdom is a project, combining ethnographic research methods started by Prof. Kate Fletcher, with design process, conveying stories and experiences related to usage of clothes. See http://localwisdom.info/

Figure 10. Hedonic consumption of fashion victims (e.n.).
Design and Illustration: Kardelen Aysel

Hedonic Consumption and Illusion of Happiness: Can We Slow Down?
Nesrin Turkmen

Introduction: from production society to consumption society

The picture painted as a result of fast-moving consumption and dedifferentiation brought along by the process of globalization signals to us that we need to slow down today. As an academician with theoretical and artistic studies in the fields of textile design and sustainability, in the chapter I have prepared for this book, I would like to discuss about the concept of Slow Fashion in terms of present living modes, which has been characterized with loss of meaning, aspects conflicting with happiness and to approach the issue from the perspective of happiness oriented positive design suggesting an alternative path for fast-moving consumption dead-end with regards to design. By studying Slow Fashion movement in terms of positive psychology, I try to find an answer to the question, "Can happiness oriented designs create a space for themselves in the fashion industry with slow fashion?"

We may say that ideal modes of living which emerged as a compound of different priorities, acceptances and values, have changed from past to present with effects of processes that societies underwent. While these priorities in pre-industrial societies were natural life, meeting needs through natural means, making do; in industrial societies they have become marketing labor, production for market places, working harder and saving. In the social phase after the 21st century, working and production gave their place to spending and consumption. In the modern capitalist market, power establishes the methods of influencing, inducing and controlling people via spending and consumption

(Şentürk, 2008.) The capitalist system can proceed on its way by providing continuity of production, and the continuity of production depends on the continuity of consumption.

Early 20th century has witnessed the birth of occupations like design, marketing and advertising which are focused on sales of consumption goods in increasing quantity and variety. The appearance of the concept of consumerism in this process is not only related to institutional alteration; but it also includes changes in attitudes and behaviors. The way of consumption today, rather than meeting the needs of people, has become an indicator useful for determining their positions within the society (Çetinkaya, 1992). Status of individuals within the society are defined with things they consume and fashion is the common ground of the system.

Pursuit of happiness in modern society

When considered from a sociological perspective, we can argue that on the one hand social structure increases happiness, on the other hand it deprives people of this. Evidences (Lyubomirsky vd., 2006) indicating that there is an influential relationship between happiness and self-respect, support the idea that societies encouraging self-respect also encourage happiness. In addition, researches of positive psychology defending that humans need financial power at a certain level in order to be happy indicate that majority of the present societies describe themselves as happy (Myers, 2000). On the other hand, there are findings concerning that today's social structure deprive individuals of happiness. With reference to findings that the modern human's social relationships are weaker than former generations, some researchers support the assertion that individualism and emphasis on self-respect increase egocentrism and ignore the needs of others (Mauss and others, 2012). Social psychologist Baumeister, in his work called Meanings of Life (1991), defines today's life with loss of meaning. Collectivism and religious values which give way to personal values have begun to deprive individuals of the intuition related to meaning and purpose of life; while contributing to the society by using their skills, belonging and close social relations are the most basic needs of individuals, the feeling of insignificance nowadays when many societies are coping with unemployment figures involves negative effects in terms of happiness of consumers (Figure 10.1.).

Figure 10.1. Hedonic illusions of happiness create individuals getting temporary satisfactions as they have more and "those they don't deserve" most of the time (e.n.). Design and Illustration: Kardelen Aysel.

Despite the noticeable rise in living standards of modern-day, there are some doubts about whether we are much happier or not today. When the concept of "happiness" that people run after, a final destination they want to reach, is discussed in this context, there are also opinions highlighting that happiness remained the same in the historical process (and even gradually decreased) versus theories emphasizing that there is an obvious increase in happiness. According to one of these opinions, there is a limit because of the nature of one's happiness and the level of happiness does not change in time; happiness may decrease under difficult conditions, later on it may turn back to the equilibrium level but when standards of living rise, the level of happiness cannot go beyond the equilibrium level (Cummins, 2010).

According to another approach, in modern society, due to negative effects of modernization, the level of happiness has gradually decreased. The most significant one of findings supporting the approach of negative effects of modernization on happiness has been put forth in Easterlin's studies. Richard

Easterlin is one of the leading names in this field carrying out studies in development economics, and in his study published in 1974, he demonstrated that average happiness level remained at the same degree despite the fact that income per capita in the US increased twice after the Second World War until the midst of 1970s. This situation called as "Easterlin Paradox" inferred that it was essential that welfare policies which brought growth into the forefront be reviewed seriously (Easterlin, 1974). Recent data belonging to the US prove that the situation has not changed (Easterlin, 1974). While real income per capita nearly doubled between the years of 1973 and 2004, no tendency in the increase of happiness level was observed (Clark et.al., 2008). In other words, increasing income did not cause an increase in happiness herewith. In contrast with opinions attributing increase in happiness after a certain subsistence-level to friends and good family life rather than income, there are also opinions underlining that factors such as comparisons of income, expectations and adaptation have an important role in explaining this paradox (Frey and Stutzer, 2002).

At the present time "happiness" has an important place in economy and the number of studies carried out under the name of the field of "economics of happiness" have been increasing rapidly. Economic determinants of happiness, economic policies towards increasing happiness and effects of policies to be implemented on happiness fall into the center of these studies. Today concepts of happiness or subjective well-being that have started to be included in indices as welfare criteria along with factors such as environmental awareness, education, etc. have become the research object in the field of positive psychology which is concerned with researches on what makes humans happy and what they perceive good in life. In recent years these studies have spread also into the field of design and the concept called as "positive designs" has emerged.

Positive designs for happiness

There are direct and indirect effects of products on the humans' behavior types and their experiencing the world. The effect the designer produces with the product occurs in two different levels (Fokkinga et.al., 2014). The first level happening between the user and the product is related to how the product is perceived and used; the second level is behaviors and experiences that the product makes possible and assists. Happiness/well-being/ welfare-driven designs are also defined as positive designs focus on the way of products' interaction with the user, with reference to it, on total effects as previously mentioned rather than their technical details. And this requires designers to determine their goals from the very beginning; that is to say, to think about experiences and effects designs are to cause at the first step.

Martin Seligman, American psychologist, educator, writer and known as the founder of the field of Positive Psychology, in his book called *Flourish* (2011: p.20) says that:

> "Duty of positive psychology is not to indicate or describe or determine what to really do for a person to be happy. This, as well as being an important opportunity in terms of effects, requires a responsibility as well".

We can define the idea of happiness and welfare-driven designs as an enterprise supporting humans' development and better living conditions. Although there are various definitions and discussions about what creates happiness, we may acknowledge that basically happiness is the compound of our experiences related to our pleasures and goals (Dolan 2014). At the end of the day, the struggle to be gone through in terms of design will be related to designing of products or services, providing an opportunity for experiences that are enjoyable as well as meaningful for people.

Many studies support the assertion that things we do offer longer lasting happiness than things we own; in other words, instead of "things" with material values, we should gain experiences to be happier (Nicolao, Irwin and Goodman, 2009). The mechanism explaining the state of being temporarily happy created by owning materials, that is to say, "Hedonic Adaptation" can be explained with the human being's ability to be able to adjust to the latest (Frederick and Loewenstein, 1999). No matter how much we are rolling in the dough, after some time our happiness will decrease to a basic level; and this will oblige us to the behavior of ever-growing possession in order to reach the same level of happiness. This hedonistic adaptation effect developing on the act of buying is explained with the treadmill metaphor; no matter how much we run, in reality we do not get anywhere (Brickman and Campbell, 1971). This effect may be a partial answer to the question of why materialistic people do not feel happier in comparison to less materialistic ones.

However, even if we accept that happy making designs are related to activities and experiences providing happiness, we may not answer easily what this means for design processes and designers. The reason is that sometimes this difference between experiences and buying may not be very accurate; buying products that promote experiences can create a sense of happiness close to the one felt by gaining experiences (Guevvara and Howell, 2015).

According to Desmet and Pohlmeyer's definition, who have studies in the fields of human-product interaction and positive design, three basic compounds of happiness-oriented designs are pleasure-oriented designs, personal goal-oriented designs, and value-oriented designs. That is to say, for us products might be things giving answers to questions of "Do I enjoy life?", "Do I lead a life as I wish?", "Am I a responsible person with values?" (2013).

Products focusing on our seeking pleasure might have different effects; the most distinctive one of these is their potentials to be able to be a delight directly with their texture, smell, color and labor. And they do this with what they symbolize or represent. As for individualistic goals, while they change from person to person and in time, it is a great source of happiness to work in line with these goals or to attain these goals (Lyubomirsy, 2007). The most important reason of this is creating a sense of meaning and purpose inside us and being a driving force for our daily lives. Some products, reminding us of our past experiences and gains, may be a source of a driving force in order to reach our goals in the future. How we reach our goals is as important as they are, isn't it? At this point our values step in. Undoubtedly, our values are as important as our goals to be able to feel happy. Concepts of value and virtue are the third important condition of happiness and welfare-driven designs. In this context we can say that virtuousness, independently of the consequence, is related to moral or ethical values. Design can provide creation of conditions needed for raising and shaping virtuous behaviors (Peterson and Seligman, 2004); it does that with daily products surrounding our environment, with buildings and services and not only designs made by aiming at these concepts influence individuals but they also gradually influence broader societies.

It is definitely true that in many ways design is an effective power for coming to a desired result but the individual has responsibility about the way of behavior and results to be obtained. For example, users preferring to use products gained with ethical production principles, being members of sharing societies, supporting local producers or adopting slow design products can be considered as examples supporting some values by heading towards correct designs and products (Desmet and Pohlymeyer, 2013). Designs and systems, promoting happiness for humans and establishing a sustainable relationship with their habitat, will be a driving force for their users in the beginning, these values internalized after some time will be a part of users. Thus, we can say that correctly built designs and services will be resources to assist people to live feeling happier in societies consisting of responsible and active individuals.

Can happiness-oriented design open a self-space for slow fashion movement in the fashion industry?

Growth of fast fashion and concordantly the rise in clothing consumption take part at the core of many ecological and ethical problems in the fashion industry. Recent researches indicate that utilization rate is unsustainable especially in North America; for instance, every year the amount of textile thrown away in the city of New York is 2.000.000 tons, 45% of these can be used in a way, and 10% of these are wearable products (Flynn, 2014).

We can define the phenomenon of consumption as a process, but not with only one product (Corbet, 2006), our desire for consumption steers companies into constantly producing the latest or the best which in turn stirs in consumers the feeling of discarding the old and being in need of the latest and the best products. The system, called as fast fashion and forging hedonic consumption habits, is an unsustainable industry with a high production and consumption rate, characterized with the production of fashionable and cheap clothing. Not only does the adjective "fast" mentioned here refer to the concept of rapidness but also has a signification of means used for output and profit growth (Fletcher, 2010). This speed obsession in our economy puts emphasis on quantity instead of quality. "Fast" also refers to the objective of the product with a short lifetime that, on this road set out with this goal, instead of material quality designers focus on catching up with trends as it makes production possible at low price range.

Slow Fashion Movement developing against fast fashion as a result of opening destructive effects of textile industry and especially of clothing production and consumption up into discussion in terms of sustainability is an important initiative for the fashion industry. Although concepts of "Slow Fashion" and "Environmentally Sustainable Fashion" are not the same things, it can be stated that Slow Fashion is indirectly an eco-friendly approach as a matter of causing less resource consumption and less waste production due to making production in small quantities (Cline, 2012). This movement also suggests a type of production increasing quality of work and life for workers in the industry, that is to decrease in time the pressure that competition brings. This slowness has effects reflecting from production process onto production quality but Slow Fashion requires a more holistic view over the issue of not only how we should produce but also how we should consume. A sustainable product become unsustainable as a result of swiftly disposing products, made of eco-friendly materials and made through eco-friendly production methods, after using only a few times (Le Blanc, 2012). In Slow Fashion not only is quality a goal in physical sense, but also a goal to be reached in terms of design. It can be said that high quality design products are also products with permanence in terms of style. Products designed to be affected less from promiscuous fashion trends and made of quality materials will undoubtedly be used for a longer time. With this movement consumers will be able to focus on their different needs nourishing their personal identities, not on temporary, rapidly changing fashion trends that everybody chases (Figure.9.2).

One of the keys to success in design is to establish a bond between the consumer and the designer and this bond can be created as much as the designer can balance between what is rational and functional and what is natural and sensational. Slow Fashion's power to be able to include the user in the process of production may enable them to create a bond between the product and the producer; and this helps the user to develop a more responsible viewpoint by raising their level of consciousness about production phases of the product intended to be bought.

Figure 10.2. While temporary fashion trends encourage consumers to buy "new" clothes that they don't need, most of the time they lure them into the trap of dedifferentiation (e.n.). Design and Illustration: Kardelen Aysel.

Slow Fashion, consumers of which have a tendency to look at the issue of clothing industry's effects on both the producer and communities related to this field from a broader perspective of sustainability, can be considered to be a more comprehensive movement in this respect when compared to environmental sustainability. Supporters of slow fashion are users not much influenced by external sources, caring more about personal needs, and they create a consumer profile attaching importance to social responsibility entrepreneurship of brands related to individual consumer demands. Consumers adopting this movement are people preferring well-known brands, ready to pay high price for high quality but in need of which is very different and unique (Lin, 2017); however, another significant peculiarity of this consumer group preferring sustainable products not as an indication of their environmental awareness but considering them as an answer to personal needs and running after which is valuable, is that they have strong ties with social media.

In terms of consumer behaviors, the relationship between the consumer and the creator of the product, and the emotional bond between the consumer and the product are key components for Slow Fashion. These components direct the consumer to buy longer lasting products and to dispose of lower number of products. In other words, awareness of the consumer and sense of responsibility are significant factors directing Slow Fashion consumer. Consumers feeling responsible for results to come out due to their buying preferences will make them support Slow Fashion movement (Antonett and Maklan, 2014: p.122).

Conclusion

Slow Fashion Movement which provides a new perspective in today's world in which the role of design in people's happiness is questioned looks promising as a movement to sprout and spread values that positive designs in textile and fashion industry represent with an understanding of sustainable and responsible design. It seems that the most crucial point with regard to adopting of and spreading Slow Fashion Movement among people is its achievement in leading young consumers at the beginning of their lives about the issue of developing perspectives and habits lasting for a lifetime to an eco-friendly and sustainable consumption concept.

While fashion takes place at the core of our culture, influencing our relations, aesthetical needs and our sense of identity, on the other hand indifference of textile and fashion industry to ethical and environmental problems has a harmful effect in social and ecological sense; effects of feeling of insecurity, class oppression, consumption and standardization are increasingly seen on people due to the effect of globalization. Relations between fashion and consumption are undoubtedly violating with sustainability goals but we can create ideal production opportunities in order to minimize negative effects of fashion and prefer a sense of design in which there is an interaction between producers and users. This is a progress which is able to change our practice of producing things doing harm to the health of society and environment and a separation point of a culture defined with materialistic consumption and of a culture in which material and spiritual products help us to understand the world, each others and ourselves. The question "Can we really slow down?" will continue to be a question to be discussed for seeking an answer with researches and foresights of anthropologists, sociologists, and economists along with design theoreticians within the next years.

Bibliography

Antonetti, P. and Maklan, S. (2014). Feelings that make a difference: how guilt and pride convince consumers of the effectiveness of sustainable consumption choices. *Journal of Business Ethics*, 124(1), p. 117-134.

Baumeister, R. F. (1991). *Meanings of life*. New York, Guilford Press.

Bayhan, V. (2011). Tüketim Toplumunda Bireyin Ontolojik Mottosu: "Tüketiyorum öyleyse varım". *Sosyoloji Konferansları Dergisi*. Ed. 43.

Brickman, P.ve Campbell, D. T. (1971) Hedonic relativism and planning the good society,[İçinde] Appley, M. H. (Ed), *Adaptation level theory: a symposium*. New York, Academic Press, p. 278-302

Clark, A. E., Frijters, P. ve Shields, M. A. (2008) Relative Income, Happiness, and Utility: An Explanation for the Easterlin Paradox and Other Puzzles, Journal of Economic Literature, Vol. 46, No. 1, p. 95-144

Cline, Elizabeth L. (2012) Overdressed: *The Shockingly High Cost of Cheap Fashion*. New York, Penguin Group.

Corbett, J. B. (2006) *Communicating nature: How we create and understand environmental messages*. Washington, D.C., Island Press.

Cummins, R. A. (2010) Subjective wellbeing, homeostatically protected mood and depression: A synthesis. *Journal of Happiness* Studies, 11

Çetinkaya, Y. (1992) *Reklamcılık*. İstanbul, Ağaç Yay., p.85.

Desmet, P. M. A.ve Pohlmeyer, A. E. (2013) Positive design: an introduction to design for subjective well-being, *International Journal of Design*, Vol 7, No 3, p. 5-19

Dolan, P. (2014) *Happiness by design: change what you do, not what you think.*, London, UK, Hudson Street Press

Easterlin, R. (1974) *Does economic growth improve the human lot?* .Some empirical evidence. University of Pennsylvenia. [Online Source]

http://graphics8.nytimes.com/images/2008/04/16/business/Easterlin1974.pdf. [Accessed 28 August 2018]

Guevarra, D. A.ve Howell, R. T. (2015) To have in order to do: exploring the effects of consuming experiential products on well-being, *Journal of Consumer Psychology*. Vol 25, No 1, p. 28–41

Fletcher, K. (2010). Slow fashion: an invitation for systems change. Fashion Practice: The Journal of Design, Creative Process & the Fashion Industry, 2(2).

Flynn, K.(2014) (Textile recycling: A for-profit startup success among controversy.*Forbes*. [Online Source] http://www.forbes.com/sites/ kerryflynn/2014/08/27/textile-recycling-a-for-profitstartup-success-among-controversy/ [Accessed 27 August 2014]

Fokkinga, S. F., Hekkert, P., Desmet, P. M. A. and Özcan, E. (2014) "From product to effect:towards a human-centered model of product impact", Proceedings of Design Research Society's 2014 Conference: Design's Big Debates, Lim, Y.-

K., Niedderer, K., Redström, J., Stolterman, E., & Valtonen, A. (eds), Umeå, Sweden: Umeå Institute of Design, Umeå University. p. 3-7.

Frederick, S. & Loewenstein, G. (1999) Hedonic adaptation[İçinde] Kahneman, D., Diener, E. & Schwarz, N. (Eds), Well-being: *The foundations of hedonic psychology.* New York, Russell Sage Foundation, p. 302-329.

Frey, B.S. and Stutzer, A. (2002) What Can Economists Learn from Happiness Research?. *Journal of Economic Literature* 40 (2), p. 402-435.

LeBlanc, S. (2012) Sustainable Fashion Design: Oxymoron No More. [Online Source] http://www.bsr.org/en/our-insights/report-view/sustainable-fashion-design-oxymoron-no-more]. [Accessed 29 November 2012]

Liu, C. (2017)"Who Buys Slow Fashion: A Study of Lifestyle Characteristics and Motivating Factors among Young Consumers" ,International Textile and Apparel Association (ITAA) Annual Conference Proceedings,ITAA Proceedings, St. Petersburg, Florida, ABD.#74.

Lyubomirsky, S. (2007) *The how of happiness.* London, UK, Piatkus, Lyubomirsky, S., Tkach, C., and DiMatteo, M. R. (2006). What are the differences between happiness and self-esteem. *Social Indicators Research Journal* , 78(3), p. 363-404.

Mauss, I. B., Savino, N. S., Anderson, C. L., Weisbuch, M., Tamir, M., and Laudenslager, M. L. (2012). T*he pursuit of happiness can be lonely. Emotion,* 12(5), p. 908-912.

Nicolao, L., Irwin, J. R. & Goodman, J. K. (2009) Happiness for sale: do experiential purchases make consumers happier than material purchases?. *Journal of Consumer Research,* Vol 36, p. 188-198.

Peterson, C. and Seligman, M. E. (2004) *Character strengths and virtues: a handbook and classification.* New York, Oxford University Press

Pohlmeyer, A.E. and Desmet, P.M.A. (2017) From good to the greater good. [In] Chapmani J. (Ed.) *The Routledge handbook of sustainable product design.* Londan, Routledge. p.469-486.

Seligman, M. E. P. (2011) *Flourish.* New York,Free Press,

Şentürk, Ü.(2008) Modern Kontrol: Tüketim. C.Ü. *Sosyal Bilimler Dergisi.* Aralık 2008., Vol: 32. No:2, p. 221-239.

Veenhoven, R.ve Dumludağ, D. (2015) *İktisat ve Mutluluk. İktisat ve Toplum Dergisi,* No: 58, p. 46-51.

Figure 11. The speed of accessing to fashion (e.n.).
Design and Illustration: Kardelen Aysel

The Chronopolitics of Slow Fashion
Otto von Busch

Introduction

Fashion and time are intricately intertwined, yet they also have a complicated relationship, as fashion somehow defines a certain time as much as it cuts through time itself. Philosopher Giorgio Agamben unpacks this in his essay "What is the contemporary?":

> "Fashion can be defined as the introduction into time of a peculiar discontinuity that divides it according to its relevance or irrelevance, [...] But if we try to objectify and fix this caesura within chronological time, it reveals itself as ungraspable [...] the "now", the kairos of fashion is ungraspable: the phrase, "I am in this instant in fashion" is contradictory, because the moment in which the subject pronounces it, he is already out of fashion."
>
> (Agamben 2009: p. 49)

While we may organize the succession of styles in chronological order, putting seasons after each other, their anticipatory charge, intensity and social context easily slip through our nets. Thus trying to manipulate the aspect of time in fashion is in itself an endeavor steeped in paradoxes, and impeding the flow of fashion is a bit like trying to switch off time by causing train-delays.

The design of time

The struggle over time within the regime of fashion echoes the struggle between individual time and standardized time at the advent of the telegraphs and railroads. Where before the invention of the telegraph and railroad each city would have its own time, it was the emerging fast travel of information and people between cities that pushed the need to standardize time across whole regions and countries. Just like the pendulum clocks have revolutionized the measurement of time throughout the day (not only in daylight), the technological advance of movement required new concepts of time to be implemented and enforced. As highlighted in his book on the connection between everyday life and innovation, Steven Johnson (2014: p.180) points out how time is not neutral but serves technological and economic functions of society. The way we experience time today has very little to do with measuring the accurate position of sun on the sky; time is not about the actions of celestial bodies, but about shaping human action and bodies.

A similar disconnect as between time and the sun, we can today experience in the disconnect between the seasons of fashion and the actions of human consumption. Not only do fashion seasons exist in any relevant way after the continuous push of new collections and online shopping, but the patterns of consumption have emerged as tools of present continuous change and updates of identity. "In a society in which design has taken over the function of religion," cultural theorist Boris Groys (2008) posits, "self-design becomes a creed." As the tools for designing, producing and disseminating the self, we are drawn to continuously broadcast ourselves. In a similar vein, cultural critic Byung-Chul Han (2015: p.49) argues we are no longer human "subjects" who submit to the order of society, but instead we have become "projects" – individual processes of perpetual becoming and achievement. Whereas the subject could remain within its own body, the project is an auto-exploitative process of conquering time itself, continually affirming its own transgression and metamorphosis; always in competition to outperform its peers and rivals. Sociologist Zygmunt Bauman draws similar conclusions and he sees fashion as a perpetuum mobile, a "self-feeding, self-sustaining, self-propelling and self-invigorating process" (Bauman, 2010: p.55). In competitive capitalist societies, fashion is a self-perpetuating process fused into the fabric of the current social order (Figure 11.1). Instead, fashion is an energy far beyond equilibrium, as it thrives in social frictions and tensions. As Bauman (2010) notes, it cannot exist in a condition of stable state, as it needs to be perpetually renegotiated (p.58). He continues;

"The perpetuum mobile of fashion is thereby the dedicated, dexterous and seasoned destroyer of all and any standstill. Fashion casts lifestyles in the mode of permanent and principally un-finishable revolution."

(Bauman 2010: 58)

Figure 11.1 The cycle of fashion is often nurtured by the recollection of old styles. In this mechanism, temporality defines the present not with the "new", but always with the "renewed" (e.n.). Design and Illustration: Kardelen Aysel

Thus the concept of slow fashion does not emerge from a vacuum. For example, the idea of slow food answers to the normalized condition of fast food, that is, that all food today is in some way fast. Even the average cookbook for the use of a slow cooker announces to the reader how many minutes it takes to prepare and rationalizes how the cook can leave the machine cooking while doing something more important – perhaps meditate or do yoga. In a similar vein, slow fashion answers to fast fashion. Today all fashion is fast in the way that all brands and stores continually minimize the time between their seasons and "drops" of new stuff. No consumer can be left waiting, as that is a potentially lost customer. The important motto is the same: keep the customers continually entertained and feed their anticipation. Time, information and excitement are three rivers flowing out through the same delta called fashion.

175

The distribution of speed

Slowness is not only about speed. Just as with slow food and slow design, behind the concept of slowness rests a romanticized idea of a mindful and higher subjectivity. The celebration of slowness makes the implicit claim that speed is something made in haste and without reflection, that is, with less rationality, authenticity and presence invested in the moment. In the fables the turtle is smarter than the hare. Slow and steady wins the race. Speed speaks to our sensibilities as individuals and it is a common knowledge the hasty decision is less virtuous than the slowly made one. Reflection and meditation are profound practices of the mind, whereas speed and stress are of the body, of the less-than-human.

Throughout consumerist societies slowness is today an emerging answer to problems on a planetary scale, to unsustainable consumerism and waste production. This slow narrative questions the ideal of societal progress at large in an attempt to decouple progress from consumerism to present a more possibly sustainable zero growth future. Some designers suggest we need to produce more lasting objects, things to be updated, repaired, cared for, and designs that are more emotionally durable, stuff that keep us happy longer. Slowing down the metabolism of consumerism seems to be the answer. Others aim to decouple the speed from its material consequences, thus keeping up the speed while reducing its environmental impact. For example, in William McDonough and Michael Braungart's popular "cradle to cradle" (2002) design model, the radical reuse of materials leaves nothing going to waste or to the material grave that is the dump. Following this imperative many designers today work to re-circuit their design processes from the linear to the circular use of products and materials or aim to modulate the speed in which their products are consumed.

But it is easy to forget some of the social concerns around speed. In essence, the problem is caught in the famous statement by sci-fi writer William Gibson; "The future is already here – it's just not evenly distributed." As we modulate speed and the emergence of the future it does not necessarily mean it gets more equally distributed. We must ask; who has access to which future, when, and at what pace? Or to put it more poignantly; who can afford to be slow in today's society?

If we are to examine this issue, we could approach it with cultural theorist Paul Virilio's (1986) term "dromology" in mind. To Virilio, dromology is about the logic of speed, named after the Ancient Greek noun for race or racetrack. And at the racetrack, like in politics, speed is power. Gibson's quote points to the speed through which the future arrives and that the arrow of time hits some places and people before others. Or even, as is made clear in Virilio's work, the arrow of time is a weapon wielded by some against others. In this world, fashion is more like the future predicted by Leonard Cohen in his song with that same name: "I've seen the future, brother; it is murder."

Time, chronos, is a matter of distribution and thus also a matter of politics. If politics is about the distribution of goods and agency and asks the question of who rules over whom, and in whose interest, we must ask slow fashion a similar question: what is the chronopolitics of slow fashion? Who sets the pace of fashion, for whom and in whose interest?

With its connection to the continuous arrival of the new, fashion slices up the world in continuously new ways. Yet patterns emerge where some people and places get to be called innovators, disruptors or early adopters, people who are close to the spring of time, while others are traditional or even backwards, meaning they are far from the streams of time. As sociologist and anthropologist Pierre Bourdieu (1993) argues in his analysis of the fashion industry, new brands emerge to disrupt the status quo preserved by the established brands, to bypass them by moving quicker. New emerging designers strive to get into the business, while the old ones try to keep them out, or to appropriate the new aesthetics quick enough to stay at top of the game, undermining the momentum of the newcomers. Thus a successful fashion designer manages to balance two contradictory forces; enough innovation to seem fresh, young and exciting, while simultaneously keeping customers loyal and feel the brand signifies an established position. Thus, according to this model, most high fashions steal emerging aesthetics and then sell them as expensive goods to manifest a high social position, but soon enough these signifiers become accessible to the wide masses. While such model does not explain everything it highlights the competitive nature of fashion, and as Bourdieu (1993: p.135) says, "Fashion is the latest fashion, the latest difference." Fashion as well as the future, fast or slow, reaches first the affluent, those who set the pace of time, and is then disseminated in wider circles out to the periphery and the poor.

The power to manipulate speeds

Throughout history different actors have struggled for the power over time. Castles, monuments and bunkers are structures made to slow down time, while planes, rockets and communications are made to speed up time (Virilio, 1994). Similarly, certain garments are meant to age, often those associated with old money, such as British wax jackets or exclusive handbags and jewelry. The celebration of care, repair and maintenance takes for granted that there is something valuable to slow down, that there is a quality of the now which is meant to be upheld and may gain value by its preservation. But happiness can rarely last long if one cannot afford to sustain it. Meanwhile, suffering is not meant to last, but can like any pain become chronic. It is nice and prestigious to inherit a fortune, castle or Jaguar sports car from one's parents, but few desire to inherit their parents' misfortune, poverty or homelessness (Figure 11.2).

As pointed out by Gibson, many people are left far from the future and with no control over it. They remain trapped in one continuous now not of their choosing. They do not have the means to call upon positive change but remain in perpetual suffering: for them the news offers no relief from a future that keeps undermining their struggles to move upwards or in any direction of their wishes. At the worst, these social groups need to work even more just to afford to stay afloat, or their access to the new is simply denied. In the realm of fashion, it is often the producers of fashion who remain stuck in sweatshops, areas of civil conflict of even wars, with polluted water supplies, or work as under-paid migrant laborers in the ecological cotton fields supplying the ethical slow fashion brands with sustainable materials. While slow may offer some opportunity to reflect on what is going on, the slowness itself does not necessarily mean better pay per hour or distributed control to the workers.

In order to unpack the slowness of fashion, we must come to see how the "now" is like a membrane where only the desired time passes through, where some control the flow and others have to accept the boundaries they face. The powerful wield the weapons of chronos, shoots the arrow where they want it to go. "Slow fashion" is yet another speed controlled through this membrane. As Virilio suggests, the struggle over speed is a struggle over the future. And speed is not equilibrium; it is often off-balance, and it creates turbulence as positions become unsettled and destabilized. As in any race against time there are losers and winners. Some are held back, forced into passivity, are off with a bad start. In the realm of fashion, the speed of adaption and control of materials were traditionally upheld through sumptuary laws. Historically, only certain social groups could use certain garments, colors, styles and materials. This was meant to keep social classes separate, slowing down the poor from gaining speed and momentum to enact the social roles of being equals. Today, copyrights and trademarks replace the sumptuary laws of the old days, but with effectively the same aims and consequences: holding back the poor to make sure the future stays unevenly distributed. Thus it may be no surprise slow fashion seems to be for those who do not need fashion as a tool for social mobility: those who can afford to be slow, to repair and maintain. The prestige of slowness allows a cultural signifier for those already have social positions to preserve, and have time and money to take it easy and enjoy the pleasures of reflection and meditate over their moral superiority.

Figure 11.2. The appearance of a "waif" that became the main topic with the Grunge movement in fashion, is not an image for some but a reality (e.n.). Design and Illustration: Kardelen Aysel

Rethinking the design of time in fashion

The reading of slow fashion above is of course somewhat cruel, but it highlights the tension between the fast and slow, the mobile and immobile, those with control and those left without. As more and more fashion designers strive to incorporate slow elements in their collections and processes, they must also unpack the distribution of these elements. For example, famous fashion designer Vivienne Westwood suggests we should buy less garments and spend the money on a few lasting pieces (preferably from her brand). Along the lines discussed above, Westwood (2013) points out that especially "poor people should be even more careful" – thus highlighting that the problems with fast fashion should primarily be blamed on the poor.

If the distribution of time is to be redesigned in fashion, critical designers need to examine who can access lasting garments, and if such enduring designs really work in their interest. Firstly, very few consumers can afford a garment of Westwood's design. Thus, if a slower and more ethical process means higher retail price, new financing models need to be made accessible to those with modest means. Secondly, designers must better understand the living conditions and aspirations of the social groups they work with to better unpack their desires. How can several overlapping speeds and desires coexist? Perhaps things can be complemented with experiences and abilities that can translate into social and emotional mobility, or new ways of celebration of aesthetic connectivity can be prototyped.

If we see that fashion has several speeds and metabolisms, where arrows and cycles overlap and outlive others, we also see how some groups stay on top, and enjoy their slowness, while others are forced to eat fast and cheap calories just in order to keep working their long hours. Indeed, as with eating, a healthy slow diet is today prestigious and not accessible to the masses. Instead, it is the poor who get obese on the processed and high calorie dreams of a future that will actually never reach them. Slow fashion risks not only become a practice of privilege, but also become a moral high ground of those who can afford to be reflective, enduring and craft-oriented. These may be groups of people who are powerful and can set the pace of ethical fashion, both the distribution of the "new" and the "slow". Meanwhile the poor at the periphery scavenge fast processed calories from the Internet, or chains like H&M and Zara, trying to prove their worth in the race of becoming entrepreneurs of identity and selling their abilities on the markets of perpetual achievement.

Fashion is a dream world. It is a realm of fantasy and creativity. The conundrum for designers is how it can be made more sustainable. Some dreams move slowly while others are fast, and dreams where we are without control we often experience as nightmares. So we must ask, how can we disseminate the control over the speed of fashion, while making sure the dream is also accessible to the weakest, the people the furthest from the springs of time? Can a dream like fashion be evenly distributed, can it move beyond speed towards other qualities and intensities? Yet designers must not forget the political question of slow fashion: what speed is allowed, for whom, and in whose interest?

Bibliography

Agamben, G. (2009) "What is the contemporary?" [In] *What is an Apparatus?: And Other Essays.* Stanford, Stanford University Press

Bauman, Z.(2010) "Perpetuum mobile", *Critical studies in fashion and beauty.* 1: 1, pp. 56-63.

Bourdieu, P. (1993) "Haute Couture and Haute Culture", [In] *Sociology in Question.* London, Sage.

Groys, B. (2008) The Obligation to Self-Design. E-Flux Journal #00 November 2008 [Online] http://www.e-flux.com/journal/the-obligation-to-self-design/ [Accessed 24 August 2018]

Han, B-C. (2015) *The burnout society. Stanford,*Stanford University Press

Johnson, S. (2014) *How we got to now.* New York, Riverhead

McDonough, W. and Braungart, M.(2002) *Cradle to cradle: remaking the way we make things.* New York, North Point Press.

Virilio, P. (1986) *Speed and Politics: An Essay on Dromology.*New York, Semiotext(e).

Virilio, P. (1994) *Bunker Archaeology.* New York, Princeton University Press.

Westwood, V. (2013) "Vivienne Westwood: Everyone buys too many clothes," interview in *The Telegraph*, September 16, 2013 [Online] http://fashion.telegraph.co.uk/news-features/TMG10312077/Vivienne-Westwood-Everyone-buys-too-many-clothes.html [Accessed 24 August 2018]

DESIGN/ BRAND / COLLECTIVE CASES FROM TURKEY

Design Exhibitions

"Seamless Clothes "
Sedef Acar

"Coming through Water" The exhibition of the Search of Seamless Forms, Izmir University of Economics, Faculty and Fine Arts and Design Gallery, January 2017, Izmir

Sedef Acar received Proficiency of Art degree from Dokuz Eylul University, Institute of Fine Arts, Textile and Fashion Design Department. Being an academician at the same university, she both produces garments based on the principle of slow fashion and sustainability in design. The output of her fabric focuses on seamless handmade methods as an alternative to conventional dress-making techniques. Whereas in conventional garment production process, patterns that are matching are cut and sewn, in Acar's works the piece of garment is built by transforming a simple garment into a detailed wearable artwork. Accordingly, the texture and feel of the garment are simultaneously built during the experimental forming process through the collaboration of wool. The present method based on giving shape during the process instead of conventional tailoring skills also includes "form your own garment" principle in today's world where the personalized 3D design outputs have started to provide alternatives to industrial processes.

Within the process, woven or knitted fabrics by using wool which is a natural and sustainable material turned into garment forms together with traditional felt technique and handmade workmanship; thus, outfits emerge as outputs of sharing ideas and feelings with their consumers on awareness of nature. The principle of sustainability using traditional processes, craft skills and natural materials is not only limited to the use of innovative material and method but also paves the way for sustainability through crafts and traditions. As opposed to the low cost and temporary trends of "fast fashion" garments which are squeezed between seasons of fashion industry, this alternative method enables us to design outfits likely to be transferred intergenerationally thanks to designs' high quality and natural materials using craft-based production by referring to "slow fashion".

Figure 12.1. Seamless garments, seamless forming, wool fabric, gauze, 2017

Figure 12.2. Seamless garments, seamless forming, wool fabric, gauze, 2017

"Waste Free Clothes: Upcycling"
Solen Kipoz

At this exhibition, Solen Kipoz, based on the principle of nonviolence "Ahimsa" and philosophy of "Asteya", reinterpreted the design practice she developed with the aim of giving new life to old clothes. Asteya, means "to give as much as you take", that is to say, "not stealing" in yoga philosophy. It tells us to establish a fair and transparent relationship with the past and old clothes. During the creation process in which the designer renews clothes from her own past, surprising stages appear. Based on an intuitive and craft-oriented approach rather than on conventional forming method, these stages are more important than the final product. In this process, pieces obtained by disassembling the parts of old clothes are traced and new forms are made.

A manufacturing process has been created where parts of old clothes are used without any cutting or changing the form, and it produces almost zero waste. Pieces are replaced by using a deconstructive method and become new forms as a result of seeking new meanings. In the end, the principle of Asteya springs to life by giving what one takes from the old cloth to the new one. This approach in the long run aims at establishing a slow and circular production-consumption system for realizing the value and potential confronting our irresponsible consumption that has become dominant today.

Figure 13.1a/13.1b. "Decorative Memory", woolen fabric 2 trousers, 1 dress, 1 skirt, deconstruction and silk screen printing, 2017

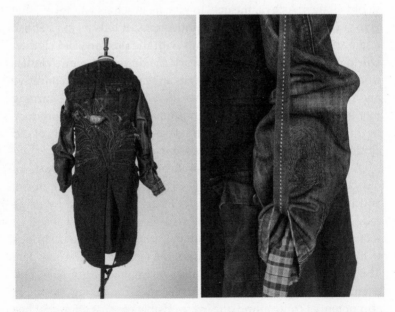

Figure 13.2a/13.2b. "Finger Print", 3 trousers (denim and non-denim fabric), 1 shirt, deconstruction, hand stitching and embroidery technique, 2017

Figure 13.3a/13.3b. "Gathering", 1 trouser, 1 jacket, 1 skirt, woolen fabric, deconstruction technique, 2017

"Un-cut Clothes"
Yuksel Sahin

"Un-cut Clothes" The Exhibition of Experimental Clothing Design, Çamurdan Art Studio/ Eskişehir- 11-16 April 2018

With this exhibition, Yuksel Sahin looks at the cutting technique which is present in our understanding of clothes. According to Şahin; "cutting" is a tailor's processing of giving shape to the fabric according to a certain measure and model. "Model" in colloquial language has a meaning that refers to design in fashion. Our understanding of clothes since the period of Westernization, when the effects of "flat pattern" cutting technique have started to be apparent, is based on simple geometric cutting technique. In this process, parts that fit the anatomic structure of the body are formed and patterns are made. The fabric which is cut according to the forming pieces are conjoined through sewing techniques and the clothing is made.

It is seen that the process of giving shape to a clothing in our traditional clothes happens with a sense of simple geometric cutting based on the width of the fabric unlike the advanced cutting techniques which involves "cutting with flat pattern". If we examine a piece of traditional clothing, we can see that all pieces are made of long rectangles and squares. Thus, when the clothing is disassembled, it is easily used in a totally different way. Şahin, with this approach, suggests an experimental paradigm of a waste free, recyclable and circular clothing production system against waste problem and fabric wastage occurring as a result of clothing cutting in the industrial fashion design system today.

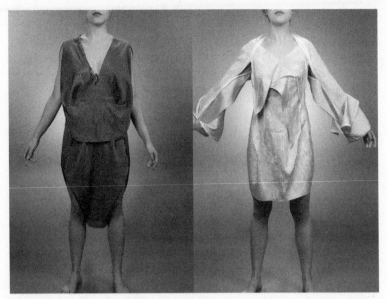

Figure 14.1. From left to right; "The soil", hand-woven, Gaziantep, Kutnu fabric, 2018

Figure 14.2. "The Sun", the technique of forming with Kutnu fabric and fabric width, 2018

Figure 14.3. "As she knows", Kutnu fabric used transversely, 2018

DESIGN/ BRAND / COLLECTIVE CASES FROM TURKEY
Slow Fashion Brands

Wearable Artistic Touches on Felt
Selçuki&Ali

Selçuki&Ali is a brand that creates works of 'The Art of Fiber' where natural raw materials like wool, silk and cashmere are used and produced with handmade methods. The brand founded by artists/designers Selçuk Gürışık and Ali Alev has been active in Istanbul since 2011. Wearable art enriched with personal touches inspired by nature applies the principles of environmental ethics and slow fashion design to works they prepare for interior-architecture objects and artistic exhibitions. Organic forms created by very special images form a 'universal visual cultural language' with their own expression by means of symbols representing timeless elegancy/delicacy. Moreover, their own design and production approach enables them to gain an effective appearance in international markets that take aim at luxury products.

In addition, their activities towards social responsibility projects like working with disabled people and art therapy activities enable them to break the established criteria and make them normless. The brand, as an alternative to art therapy; breaks new ground with practices of 'Treatment with Design and Product Making'. The outcome of increasing market demands for handmade natural designs and sustainable/slow fashion products can persuade masses in a positive way with more concrete productivity examples and increases hope towards these movements. The brand that adopts the strategy of 'today can be the tradition of tomorrow' sustains creativity by bearing the responsibility of all marks it is to leave behind.

Figure 15.1. Fiber Fusion 1 - Wool-felted silk satin ribbon and hand-twisted wool thread, 2010

Figure 15.2. Fiber Fusion 2- Silk-satin fabric trapped between hand-twisted wool threads and fiber, 2013

Figure 15.3. Fiber Fusion 3- Silk chiffon fabric appliqued with wool and silk fiber motives, 2016

Upcycled and Wearable Collage Art
Gönül Paksoy

Gönül Paksoy focuses on costume design at her atelier in Istanbul, Nisantasi since 1989, transforming old fabrics, textures and dyes and producing exclusive designs with characteristics of art pieces. Textile pieces that have at least one hundred years due to their accumulative, collecting characteristic have an important place in the process of her creation in terms of life experiences they have and in terms of either texture or color and their functional and formal effects. Paksoy's sense of design inspired by the Ottoman's textile treasure and dervish clothing is described as 'mystic'. In her textile laboratory, materials like raw wool, raw linen, raw silk, felt, velvet, ikat weaving, tinsel texture, tinsel embroidery, silk crepe, *çatma*[1] woven from natural fibers take color tones, consisting of semitones, include a little life experience and imagination of the designer and associated with her own name.

For Paksoy, who creates designs that resist to 'temporal newness', 'sustainability' is a philosophy, a way of life, and 'slowness' is a manner and a choice. Paksoy puts sustainability philosophy into practice with the process of experimental design and does not waste any stuff and any pieces of fabric. All pieces left from the process are used in the collection. As much as their visual and cultural richness, clothes designed by Paksoy are considered as "the best examples of collage art" by some critics, and have extraordinary functionality, variety and economy due to the usability of both sides. The designer who produces only one clothing from each design, considers each of her designs as a part of an extensive mosaic completing one another and communicating with each other. She does not label her clothes, as she believes they are distinguished by their uniqueness.

Figure 16.1. Sweater: All handmade, naturally dyed, silk sweater. Jacket: the approximate age of the Ottoman fabric is 150 years. Collar: Naturally dyed old velvet, 2003, (*Çatma*).

From left to right; Figure 16.2. The sleeves of a handwoven coat are made from embroidered dyed velvet. The coat is made from old, hand-woven, silk-wool blend fabric, not dyed, 2003

Figure 16.3. It can be used as a scarf or a skirt. The fabric is 60 years old. Old fabrics are two-sided and made of patchwork, 2007

Notes

1   A woven fabric with floral patterns with the use of silk threads to crate a velvety embossment in the late Ottoman period.

Clothes Created with Participatory Design
INCOMPLIT

INCOMPLIT is a fashion brand appreciating imagination, humanity, labor, water, earth, infinite harmony; while giving the importance to one side, not neglecting the other. Öykü Özgencil, founder of the brand INCOMPLIT that has been in service in Istanbul since 2015, consider it as a social innovation model in addition to its sustainability, selection of materials, and production methods. INCOMPLIT prepared a workshop program centered around only one story for 12 weeks in collaboration with NGOs that work with disadvantaged children. In order to realize this project, they took support from various artists and disciplines. In these workshops, children complete the interrupted story by fictionalizing a character, by chorusing altogether and by choreographing a dance. All these workshops are held so that they can look at the same construct in a thousand ways, develop their empathy abilities and emotional intelligence.

At the end of the three-month period, colors children wrap themselves up, figures they draw out, questions they ask, dreams, lines become the lifeline of a fashion collection with a long subtext, that is troubled but at the same time holds the key. INCOMPLIT, working with women's cooperatives and with a master who is a 30-year-experienced tailor, produces each piece in a limited number. In products, not only do dreams of children but also those of a veteran master and of women who believe in themselves lie.

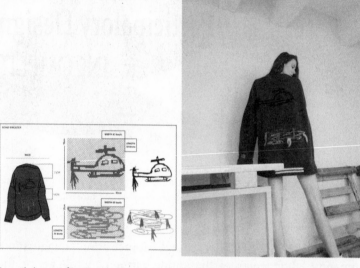

From left to right; Figure 17.1a / 17.1b. Pictures from the workshops supported by the UN-IOM (United Nations International Organization for Migration) in Gaziantep were transformed into wool cardigans, sweaters and ponchos by the Edirne housewives through these templates in the BOND- (BAG) collection, 2017

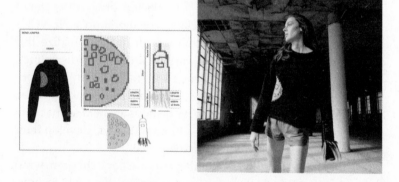

Figure 17.2a / 17.2b. Pictures from the workshops supported by the UN-IOM in Gaziantep have passed through INCOMPLIT's design approach and the hands of Edirne housewives and turned into wool cardigans, sweaters and ponchos in the BOND- (BAG) collection, 2017

Figure 17.3. In the story completion workshops supported by the United Nations-International Organization for Migration, Ali's drawing was embroidered on the Moon Sweater from the Bond collection, Gaziantep, April 23, 2017

Solidarist and DIY Design
Mandalinarossa

As an alternative to mass production and as a reaction to over consumption Mandalinarossa creates handmade and small quantity of clothing. The brand is established by Nazlı Çetiner Serinkaya who is trained as a fashion designer with knitwear specialization in FIT, New York. Since 2007 she has produced colorful, full-of-texture knitwear collections for women and children with a hand operated, non electrical knitting machine in her studio in Istanbul. For clothing collections she uses natural, recycled and overstock fabrics/yarns not to consume resources. As opposed to fast consumed and discarded children's clothing, she makes them adjustable and long lasting so they can be worn for a number of years.

By giving sewing classes and publishing online pdf sewing tutorials, she encourages people to make their own clothing. Therefore rather than a consumer object, clothing becomes something that the tailor can relate to. Through her travels to Thailand and Nepal, Serinkaya has developed a number of social responsibility projects in collaboration with communities there. In Thailand she developed a recycling project by collecting discarded plastic bags to create a sustainable income source for the mountain villagers and she conducted wildcraft workshops with children. In Nepal, she worked as an atelierista in a community kindergarten and created educational tools using recycled materials.

Figure 18.1 Triangle sweater, hand knitted

Figure 18.2 Color block sweate, hand knitting, 2015

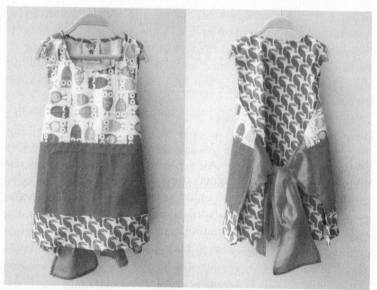

Figure 18.3. Adjustable dress for children, cotton fabric , 2015

Clothes with Stories
Reflect

Reflect, a textile-oriented design studio, has been developing social design-driven products for individuals and institutions since 2017. Edipcan Yıldız, Ece Altunmaral and Eray Erdoğan are partners of the studio that adopts the philosophy "everything you wear tells a story" and that operates with a sense of participatory design and responsible production. They believe in the power of stories that can make feelings palpable and ideas catchy. The studio carries out design processes with workshops and activities and values participation, interaction and different viewpoints. They invite all participants and users, be it an individual or institution, to become a part of the solution by fictionalizing stories centered around United Nations' Sustainability Development Policies that focus on urgent environmental, political and economic problems.

The brand, which refuses to take part in the environmental damage caused by the ready-made clothing industry, is one of the leading advocates of 'slow fashion' approach. Within this framework, where the designers use eco-friendly, organic, recycled or upcycled materials, the brand guarantees that all processes from manufacturing to distribution are conducted ethically and transparently. *Reflect* manufactures internationally certified products in limited numbers and promises durable designs with a long life against the transience of fashion. In addition to their own collections, the studio has also developed various products for organizations such as Chobani, Redbull and Tent Organization.

Figure 19.1. From the Solidarity collection, GOTS certified 100% Organic Cotton, tank embroidery on the back, 2017

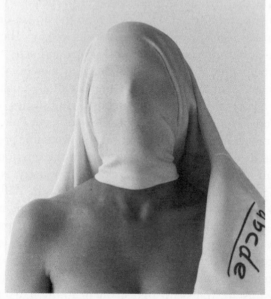

Figure 19.2. "Alphabet" from the collection YOU MADE IT, three-thread 100% cotton non raised fabric. Can be worn on both sides, sleeves are embroidered on both sides, 2018

Figure 19.3. The collection YOU MADE IT, three-thread 100% cotton raised fabric, 8 different blood groups were embroidered in 8 different places of a hoodie; "Can a red hoodie remind us that we all bleed the same?", 2018

In this collection, considering the idea of Ludwig Wittgenstein that "our world's boundaries are the boundaries of our language", "Alphabet" with Latin letters on one side and Arabic letters on the other side, designed as a result of getting inspired by a printout of art therapies held for children, encourages to think about the communication crisis a refugee goes through in the country he arrives.

Clothes Colored with Vegetal Dyes

Sat-su-ma

Sat-su-ma is a brand that produces vegetable dyed organic cotton clothes. It came out in 2014 when Özge Horasan started to weave handmade clothes made of naturally dyed fabrics that are made according to traditional formulas. In 2016, the technique of conventional dyeing was replaced with the method of cold dyeing which was more innovative, sustainable and low-energy consuming. In addition, in their collections the brand began to use organic cottons grown in the Aegean region. Clothes are sewed at a factory fairly merchandizing in a local area and then hand dyed at the studio.

Horasan, who designs clothes suitable to any time and condition, adds soft and natural colors coming from plants to simple and comfortable cuts which always provide harmony with each other in designs. Believing in a simplified way of life, she strives to make people wearing *Sat-su-ma* feel comfortable anytime and anywhere. During its creation, this slow fashion brand was nurtured by the calmness and fertility of the ancient lands in the Aegean region, which is at the same time the home of the designer. *Sat-su-ma* is one of the leading advocates of the principle "re-establish a bond with the earth and dress more refined and responsibly".

Figure 20.1. 2017 Spring/Summer Collection, organic cotton, herbal dyeing technique

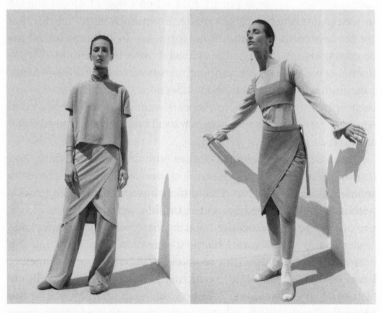

Figure 20.2. and 20.3. 2017 Spring/Summer collection, organic cotton fabric, herbal dyeing technique

A Social Sustainability Brand
Argande

The Project on Innovations for Empowerment of Women in GAP Region that has been carried out since 2008 created an urban clothing brand for women by collecting their products under the brand *Argande*. The project has been financed by the partnership of United Nations Development Programme (UNDP) and SAP Regional Development Administration (SAP RDA) and Swedish International Development Cooperation Agency (SIDA). The project aims at the participation of women in labor market, branding of Southeast Anatolia and creating new sales and marketing opportunities. Within the project's framework that is under the coordination of the fashion designer Hatice Gökçe, Turkey's leading fashion designers work in close cooperation with women in the region on a volunteer basis and prepare fashion products to be exposed for sale. Gönül Sulargil is responsible for project management, Bülent Fidan for brand consultancy and Yeşim Demir for corporate identity.

Products, coming out of women's workshops, bring together knowledge and skills of Southeast women and creativity of fashion designers. Products are marketed in various metropolis in Turkey with the slogan "Talismans Emerging from the Same Sun". The first collection of *Argande* was launched in 2009, and its collections throughout 18 seasons have been put up for sale at Mudo stores, one of the biggest ready-made clothing companies in Turkey. Due to the visibility of the cultural heritage, the project, which is based on the richness of local culture, skills, diversity and women's productivity, positions the regional economy in commercial markets and contributes to a more positive perception of the region. Argande is a slow fashion brand that creates a social sustainability model, reaches approximately 1000 women and provides employment opportunities.

Figure 21.1. 2017 autumn/winter collection, Patterned trousers made of kutnu fabric and cotton jacket, Design: Aslı Jackson, Photographer: Jerry Stolwijk, Model: Sema Şimşek

Figure 21.2 and 21.3. Cotton-embroidered jacket and a patterned skirt made of kutnu fabric; Patterned dress made of kutnu fabric, digital print, Design: Aslı Jackson, Photographer: Jerry Stolwijk, Model: Sema Şimşek

Waste Management Consultancy
Zero Design

Zero is a design and innovation studio working on practical and scalable practices of circular economy. The aim of the studio brought into action by Gülin Ölçer in 2017 is to raise awareness of private sector, academia, non-governmental organizations and individuals about circular economy and sectoral practices. The studio represents Turkey in the Circular Economy Club, the largest circular economy network in the world. It is in close relationship with ATÖLYE, a network of entrepreneurs and designers in Turkey, and European Bank for Reconstruction and Development (EBRD) supported by Sustainable Development Association (SDA), a branch of World Business Council for Sustainable Development (WBCSD) in Turkey. This cooperation aims at conveying the principals of circular economy to masses and companies. *Zero* has introduced circular economy to more than 1000 people in Turkey due to the activities, trainings, workshops and published materials on the related topic.

Zero's team of experts in product, service and system design come together with business analysts and environmental engineers in order to implement projects on measurable objectives. One of these projects is performance increasing interior surface design which has been the finalist at NIKE GRIND's competition of developing new product from textile waste held in cooperation with San Francisco based OPEN IDEO and Nike. Another one is the great data platform carried out by the collaboration of Holland and London based company Reverse Resources and Turkish textile manufacturers and fabric recycling centers. The aim of the platform is to measure textile wastes on their journey through the value chain and to transfer real-time data on waste production to the relevant brand.

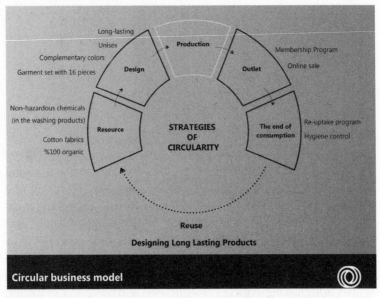

Figure 22.1. The circular business model developed by Zero Design

Figure 22.2. Acoustic tiles, flowerpots and floor coverings produced by recycling textile wastes, 2018

DESIGN/ BRAND / COLLECTIVE CASES FROM TURKEY

Activist Platforms and Collectives

Clothes Swapping
Swapping Action Platform

In order to prevent post-consumption clothes from becoming a waste in the fashion industry, swap experience initiated in 2012 in Istanbul by Nazlı Ödevci and Fulya Müftüoğlu aims at changing the consumption habits with more than 25 organized activities. In this context, the objective of Clothes Swapping Platform, which has the slogan 'Free Innovation', is to question our consumption habits shaped by the lifespan of clothes reduced to the market value and 'trendiness' and to support the solutions to change these habits. In the vicious circle of carefree consumption encouraged by the fast fashion industry, they continue to create a pile of clothes we do not use in our closet. Clothes Swapping made it possible to exchange these piles. Its goal is to make people give importance to 'usage value' instead of 'material value', to form a consciousness of responsible consumption and create a society living with sustainability awareness in general.

Swapping activities enable people to discard unused clothes and make room in their closets. In addition to that, new clothes can be obtained without paying any money upon the request. Thus, each product is one step closer to the maximum utilization potential. Clothes Swapping announces events where participation is free of charge on social media and donates unexchangeable clothes to associations and NGOs at the end of the day. Among the organizations that received donations are the Mor Çatı Women's Shelter Foundation and the Foundation for the Support of Women's Work (FSWW). The platform, which has donated more than 5000 products to this day, ensures that all of the products are used, clean and undamaged and evaluated for the benefit of women and children.

Figure 23.1. In addition to the clothes swapping activities, Giysi Takası (Clothes Swapping) platform organizes do-it-yourself workshops that encourage production.

Figure 23.2. Giysi Takası exhibits a solidarist economy model where users meet each other to swap clothes that can be preferred and used 'without spending money', Studio-X, 2018

Figure 23.3. Swap events that create a 'meeting bazaar' in various cultural venues promise a 'free' shopping experience. SALT Beyoğlu, 2012

Cultural and Collective Art Platform for Sustainable Living
CIRCUIT Istanbul

CIRCUIT Istanbul is a social and activist platform emerging as a representation of the conception of sustainable life. It came out as an idea when in 2013 Ülkü Çağlayan got to know permaculture at an off-grid training farm in South Africa. Çaglayan, having adopted a new approach with the skill of ecological design essentially embodying wisdom to turn waste into resources and realizing negative effects of her own consuming attitude on the planet's ecological design, went through a dramatic change during the time she stayed at the farm. In the same year, she founded CIRCUIT Istanbul as a center themed with a sustainable lifestyle in order to deal with the change as a value in alternative and performative ways and to convey it. CIRCUIT Istanbul, determining social participatory art practices as the language of the organization evolved to a community of art and culture in 2015, with contributions of co-founders Jessica Sim and Paul Brownlee.

The organization, apart from carrying their operation with sustainable practices, brings individuals together at creative trainings and activities. These programs are planned as part of the concepts of self-questioning, environmental awareness and consciousness of a community. With more than 300 activities, meetings and events it has organized and/or hosted, the organization aims at making inter-personal bonds, rising and supporting enterprises, expediting corporations, rising awareness and giving inspiration to individuals ready to get into the act. Sustainable design markets, secondhand markets, non-profit organizations, social entrepreneurs and launching events for sustainable brands (i.e. Fashion Revolution Turkey, Connect One Threads) and installations created and presented together are a few of them.

Figure 24.1. "Connect One Threads" Launch Event, CIRCUIT Istanbul, by organizing various activities and meetings, it equips the place with the practices of questioning (post-its for questions and answers on the walls, video presentations and various installations) and provides entertaining discussion environments with a number of tools, Çukurcuma, 2016

Figure 24.2. Circuit Istanbul Design markets are events where slow fashion formations/brands meet responsible consumers, Windmill, 2017

Figure 24.3. In the activities organized and hosted by CIRCUIT Istanbul, where individuals who think and work on sustainability come together, people are involved in a different form of social behavior and sharing while at the same time taking part in micro-actions, from Connect One Threads, Çukurcuma, 2016

A Sustainability Formation
Fashion Revolution Turkey

Fashion Revolution is an international organization that aims for sustainability of both natural and human resources in the fashion industry. It first came together in the UK following the tragedy of what has come to be known as 'The Rana Plaza Disaster'; a textile factory collapsed in Bangladesh in 2013, resulting in the death or injury of 1113 workers. Fashion Revolution began as a group of people in the fashion building, simply refusing to be part of the vicious cycle of faster and more production at the cost of the planet and human lives; prompting wearers to ask a very simple question to begin with: Who Made My Clothes? This very simple quest for transparency has gained much visibility and grew immensly over the following years, with many brands and producers responding to wearer's question by saying "We Made Your Clothes", Fashion Revolution's very own yearly transparency index, and events occuring around Fashion Revolution Day and Week (on the anniversary of Rana Plaza, April 24th) by representatives all around the world, Turkey included. Fashion Revolution Turkey represents itself in various activist events and platforms such as Circuit Istanbul and Sustainable Fashion Platform through coordination of Eda Çakmak.

Figure 25. Many sensitive fashion companies have become involved in the campaign organized by Fashion Revolution aimed at raising awareness among consumers about modern slavery in the supply chain and making manufacturers visible (e.n.). Design and Illustration: Kardelen Aysel

"Clean Clothes" Campaign Turkey
Clean and Fair Trading Platform

Clean Clothes Campaign (CCC) is an activist platform devoted to support the reinforcement of workers in global fashion and textile industries and to improve working conditions. Founded in 1989 in the Netherlands, today it operates in 15 European countries as an alliance of more than 200 institutions and unions. It is aimed at protecting women workers' rights and determining local problems and objectives in countries producing textiles. It cooperates with unions and non-governmental organizations which are members of CCC and which involve a wide range of interests and viewpoints like women's rights, consumers' advocacy and decreasing poverty. Considering the fact that globally all workers have rights to demand equal, good and fair working conditions and to be informed about their statutory rights without discrimination - of age, nationality, juridical and labor status, gender etc. - it instructs textile workers and supports them in their actions.

It endeavors to make firms transparent by preventing the problem of subcontractor posed in many supplier countries, including Turkey, and by controlling manufacture and supply conditions. While workers struggle for their rights and demands for better working conditions under the leadership of organized campaigns, members of Clean Clothes train and mobilize consumers to put pressure on firms and lobby governments and companies to provide a direct support of solidarity to workers. Within this framework, in Turkey, Clean Clothes under the coordination of Aldulhalim Demir have helped to improve working conditions, and charging and have conducted activities to improve health conditions in textile manufacturing. For example, they contributed to the recognition of silicosis by the Ministry of Health. Silicosis is a disease which is progressed in time as a result of the damage caused in lungs during denim sanding.

https://cleanclothes.org/ and http://www.temizgiysi.org/tag/clean-clothes-campaign-turkey/

Figure 26. Clean Clothes usually organizes campaigns together with consumers in front of the stores of producing companies from which textile workers need to claim their rights (e.n.).
Design and Illustration: Kardelen Aysel

Sustainable Fashion Platform (SFP)
Independent Collective

Sustainable Fashion Platform is an independent platform aimed at creating a socially and environmentally sensitive textile and fashion ecosystem and sharing knowledge, experiences and ideas. The platform includes institutions and people who carry out studies in the field of fashion and/or sustainability and who have the motivation to create a positive effect in this field. It aims at spreading the phenomenon of sustainable fashion in Turkey by providing the opportunity to all shareholders in the sector to meet on a common ground and share knowledge/opinions/experiences.

SFP, which acts as an open library with its activities, increases the level of knowledge about sustainable fashion in the sector, enables concrete people to take concrete steps to become ambassadors of change and brings together independent individuals and organizations to achieve a better transformation through a joint action in fashion and textile ecosystem.

Established at the end of 2017 and with the first event in Istanbul launched in June 2018, the institutions and persons who have provided resources for the establishment of the platform are as follows: Bükra Kalaycı, Eda Çakmak-Fashion Revolution Turkey, Edipcan Yıldız-Reflect, Gülin Ölçer-Zero Design, Irem Yanpar Cosdan-Yesilyama.com, Nazlı Ödevci-Giysi Takası (Clothes Swapping), Nermin Köse-Away Denim, Öykü Özgencil-INCOMPLIT, Pınar Öncel-Surdurulebiliryasam.tv, Refik Çolakoglu-fashionizer.com, Ülkü Çağlayan-Circuit Istanbul.

https://www.facebook.com/surdurulebilirmodaplatformu/
https://www.instagram.com/surdurulebilirmodaplatformu/

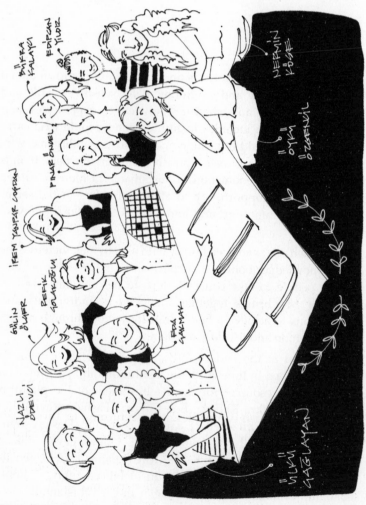

Figure 27. Sustainable Fashion Platform (e.n.).
Design and Illustration: Kardelen Aysel

Biographies of Contributing Authors

 **Duygu Atalay** currently works as an Assistant Professor in Textile and Fashion Design Department at Beykent University. She graduated as salutatorian of her faculty in 2007 from Izmir University of Economics, Department of Fashion Design. In 2009, she completed her Master's Degree in Fashion and Textile Design at Istituto Europeo di Design in Italy and collaborated with Puma on her graduation project. After her graduation, she started working at the design office of Guido Di Riccio located in Milan. She developed collections for Italian womenswear, menswear and childrenswear brands. She also worked as a freelance designer for Dutch, Austrian and Turkish companies. After returning to Turkey, she started studying for her second master's degree in Design Studies Program at Izmir University of Economics, where she also served as a research assistant for 3 years. In 2014/2015 academic year, she worked as a lecturer at Arel University. Since 2016, she has been giving lectures at Beykent University. Her research areas include sustainability, craft centered design, cultural identity and women's studies.

Otto von Busch is Associate Professor of Integrated Design at Parsons, The New School for Design. He holds a Ph.D. in design from the School of Design and Craft at the University of Gothenburg, Sweden, and was previously Professor of Textiles at Konstfack, Stockholm. He has a background in arts, craft, design and theory and many of his projects explore how design, and especially fashion, can mobilize community capabilities through collaborative craft and social activism. He has published articles in The Design Journal, Critical Studies in Fashion and Beauty, Fashion Practice, CoDesign Journal, The Journal of Modern Craft, Textile Cloth and Culture, Craft Research, Organizational Aesthetics, Creative Industries Journal & Journal for Artistic Research. His book chapters on design activism are part of The Routledge Handbook of Sustainable Product Design (2017), The Routledge Companion to Design Research (2015), The Routledge Handbook of Sustainability and Fashion (2014), as well as other design anthologies.

Hazel Clark is Professor of Design Studies and Fashion Studies at Parsons School of Design, The New School, New York. She has taught and researched in the UK, Europe, Asia, Australia, and the USA. Her interest in fashion, textiles, design, culture and the everyday have resulted in a number of co-edited publications, including: Old Clothes New Looks: Second Hand Fashion (2005) with Alexandra Palmer; The Fabric of Cultures: Fashion, Identity and Globalization (2009) with Eugenia Paulicelli; Design Studies: A Reader (2009) with David Brody; The Handbook of Textile Cultures (2016) with Janis Jeffries and Diana Wood-Conroy, and the co-authored Fashion and Everyday Life: London and New York (2018) with Cheryl Buckley. In 2018 she also co-edited Fashion Curating: Critical Practice in the Museum and Beyond wih Annamari Vanska, and co-curated the exhibition fashion after Fashion with Ilari Laamanen at the Museum of Arts and Design, New York.

 **Irem Yanpar Cosdan** completed her Bachelor's Degree at Ege University, Department of Textile Engineering, and Master's Degree at Galatasaray University, Department of Management. Getting familiar with sustainable textile at École Nationale Supérieure des Arts et Industries Textiles in France in the last term of the university, she carried on studies about the usage of natural fibers in composite materials. She is experienced in textile, in the fields of purchasing, product development, supply chain and e-commerce and has been working in private sector since 2010. On her website yesilyama.com, which she created to raise awareness about sustainable fashion, she writes articles on environmental and social impacts of the textile industry. In Turkey, she is a founding member of Sustainable Fashion Platform that aims at the creation of a textile and fashion ecosystem responsive to the planet and the society.

 **Alex Esculapio** is a PhD candidate and lecturer at University of Brighton. Their doctoral research considers the concept of emotional durability in design and assesses its implications for contemporary fashion history, theory and practice. Alex's work has been published in Fashion Theory, The International Journal of Fashion Studies, The Journal of Design Strategies, Vestoj and Fashion Projects. They have also contributed to the edited volumes Just Fashion: Critical Cases of Social Justice In Fashion (2012) and The Fashion Condition (2014).

 **Erica de Greef** is a fashion theorist and curator. Erica is the co-founder of the African Fashion Research Institute [AFRI] that serves as a platform for showcasing the politics, poetics and power of African fashion. Prior to this, Erica lectured at LISOF School of Fashion in Johannesburg for fourteen years, where she promoted critical

fashion knowledge with a strong local content, affording the development of a local fashion understanding through innovative, interdisciplinary research projects and exhibitions. These projects engaged notions of dress, history, society and identity. Erica completed her PhD in African Studies (University of Cape Town) in 2018, in which she investigated the complex challenges of, and opportunities for, South African museums to work with their dress/fashion collections to prompt transformation, engage new audiences and address archival silences. Erica is currently Co-Chair of the Research Collective for Decolonising Fashion (RCDF) and Senior Curator at the Large: Fashion Zeitz MOCAA, Cape Town.

Alison Gwilt is a fashion design researcher, author and consultant. She explores and promotes a range of innovative design methods and approaches that enable the fashion and textiles community, from educators, to producers, and consumers, to adopt more sustainable, circular and ethical practices. Her work focuses on the use of positive/sustainable design interventions that challenge the current production and consumption paradigm. Alison's books include *Shaping Sustainable Fashion* (2011), *A Practical Guide to Sustainable Fashion* (2014), *Fashion Design for Living* (2015) and *Global Perspectives on Sustainable Fashion* (2019). Alison holds a PhD from RMIT University, Melbourne and a BA (Hons) Fashion & Textiles Design from Central St Martins College of Art in London, and she has worked in academia in the UK, New Zealand and Australia. Following her role as Reader in Fashion and Sustainability at Sheffield Hallam University, UK, Alison relocated to Australia in 2017 where she is Associate Professor in Design at the University of New South Wales, in Sydney.

Alastair Fuad-Luke is a design facilitator, educator, writer and activist. His books include Agents of Alternatives (co-edited), Design Activism, and The Eco-design Handbook. Presently he is Full Professor of Design Research at the Faculty of Design &

Art at the Free University of Bozen-Bolzano, Italy. Previously he was Professor of Emerging Design Practices at the School of Arts, Design and Architecture, Aalto University, Finland, exploring co-design, openness and sharing, and a Visiting Professor at the Department of Communication and Art, University of Aveiro, Portugal. Projects in recent years include Mode Uncut; a Codesign Manual, Return on Giving, for the City of Lahti, Finland; and an Eco-Innovera research project, SHIFT about how to better support eco-innovation SMEs and startups in Europe. Present research focuses on: design and resilient agri-cultures, through a network called muu-baa.org in a project entitled What Could A Farm Be?; and an open source co-e-knitting initiative.

 **Solen Kipoz** is an academic and designer working in the field of fashion studies. Since 2001 she has been an academic member of Department of Fashion and Textile Design at Izmir University of Economics where she has delivered courses on design studio, fashion theory and ethics and social responsibility in design. Associate Prof. Dr. Solen Kipoz produces publications on fashion studies and conceptual design works on ethical, social and sustainable fashion. Her book entitled *Sustainable Fashion* (2015) published in Turkish, has been influential in the path of creating an awareness on slow and ethical fashion in Turkey. Her personal exhibition *Ahimsa: The Other Life of Clothes* (2012), her installations and performances for *PortIzmir 3 International Contemporary Art Triennial* (2014), *Asteya Exhibition* (2017) and *Salvaged Leather Exhibition* (2019) are some of her notable works. The rag doll which can be produced and personalized by the user, which she designed as a part of the installation "The Legacy in the Pocket" is registered as a utility model by Turkish Patent Institute. Kipoz, co-created this project with both women communities and children and teenagers.

Sanem Odabasi was born in 1989 in Eskişehir. She graduated from Eskişehir Anadolu University, Fashion and Textile Design Department in 2010. She worked at Istanbul Fashion Academy, and as a designer for the brands Elaidi and Dilek Hanif. She was also an editor for the Trendsetter Magazine. In 2013, she studied papermaking in Italy under the scholarship granted by UNESCO and Merloni Foundation. In Lisbon, she worked at and contributed to the foundation of the HANGAR Art Center. In 2012-2014, her articles on design and fashion were published in Design Paper, which is the supplement of Radikal Newspaper. The book called *"Bir Girişimcinin Yolculuğu"* (An Entrepreneur's Journey) to which she contributed as a co-author was published in 2017 by TUBITAK Popular Science Books. Since 2015, she has worked as a research assistant at Anadolu University, Fashion and Textile Design Department. She took part in many scientific and artistic activities with her works and wrote her postgraduate thesis on sustainability. She carries on her works related to Proficiency in Art at Osmangazi University, Art and Design Department. Her fields of study are sustainable fashion, education of sustainability and the relation of art and design.

Alice Payne is Senior Lecturer in Fashion in the School of Design, Queensland University of Technology, Australia. Her research centers on environmental and social sustainability concerns throughout textile and apparel industry supply chains. Alice has examined perspectives on sustainability along the cotton value chain, the cultural and material flows of post-consumer textile waste, and design processes of mass-market product developers, independent fashion designers, and social entrepreneurs. She is co-editor of the forthcoming book *Global Perspectives on Sustainable Fashion* (Bloomsbury 2019). Alice is an award-winning designer and has exhibited in Australia and overseas. Her recent work explores speculative approaches to design for disassembly.

Yuksel Sahin received her Bachelor's Degree at Dokuz Eylul University, Fashion and Textile Design Department, and Master's Degree at Marmara University, Faculty of Fine Arts. She also studied Proficiency in Art in the Department of Textile and Fashion Design at Dokuz Eylul University, Faculty of Fine Arts. She worked as a Folklore Researcher at the Ministry of Culture. In the years of 2000-2013 she worked as an instructor and department chair at Akdeniz University, Faculty of Fine Arts, Department of Fashion and Textile. Organizing *1st International Antalya Fashion and Textile Design Biennial* in 2012, and the *1st International Fashion and Textile Design Symposium* where she carried out the positions as the president and curator of organizing committee. Since 2013, she has she worked at the Department of Fashion and Textile Design of Anadolu University. Şahin, carrying on her studies at Eskisehir Technical University, Department of Fashion and Textile Design, has held personal exhibitions in the context of textile/fiber art, took part at triennials and biennials with her works. She has published articles, papers and books concerning her field of study.

Nesrin Turkmen graduated from Dokuz Eylul University, Faculty of Medicine in 1992. In 2001, after graduating from Mimar Sinan University, Textile and Fashion Design Department, she became a research assistant at the same department. The thesis called 'Sustainability and Transformation in Terms of Textile and Fashion Design' which she wrote during her education in Proficiency in Art in Mimar Sinan University has become a study that can be characterized as a pioneer in this field. Türkmen, with her academic and artistic studies that have been developing within the scope of Sustainable Approaches in Textile, Social and Cultural Sustainability, Slow Design, and with articles, papers and solo exhibitions, has taken part in various national and international, sociocultural, sustainability-oriented projects. Now, Nesrin Turkmen works as an Associate Professor at Mimar

Sinan University, Department of Textile and Fashion, and gives lectures mainly related to subjects of Printing Design, Artistic Textile Prints and Sustainability in Terms of Textile and Fashion Design included in Undergraduate, Graduate and Proficiency in Art Programs.

INDEX

A
added value, 114, 125
aesthetic, 21, 29, 91, 108, 109, 110, 114, 154, 177
Ahimsa, 116, 126, 187, 243
alternative economies, 16, 30, 31, 124
artisanal, 86
Asteya, 121, 187
Australian fashion, 129, 133, 134, 136, 137
Autarky, 115, 116
authentic, 25, 85

B
biodiversity, 31, 152
Black Coffee, 108, 109
Benjamin, Walter, 18, 85, 86, 97, 109

C
Campo Libro, 35, 36
chronopolitics, 172,177
chronos, 131, 132, 177, 179
circular, 18, 22, 113, 119, 121, 122, 123, 176, 187, 191, 219, 220
circular consumption, 123
circular economy, 18, 22, 83, 119, 122, 153, 219

positive design, 20, 159, 162, 163, 164, 168
post-consumption, 119, 225
preconsumption, 120
propertylessness, 115, 116, 123
prosumers, 33, 38

R

Rancière, Jacques, 29
recrafting, 101, 105, 106, 108
recyclable, 191
recycling, 121, 207, 220, 221
repurposing, 64, 101, 103
responsible, 230, 233
rewilding, 37
rivers, 48, 118, 175
Rivers, 136,137

S

sensorial, 60, 67, 130
sensorial design, 114
sharing economy, 18, 19, 113, 122, 124, 125
Sinerji, 137
social sustainability, 216
solidarist, solidarity, 125, 207, 209, 227, 236
slow, 125, 130, 148, 150, 154, 159, 176, 178-181, 187
Slow Cities, 25, 27
slow design, 15, 16, 17, 20, 26-30, 33, 37, 73, 88, 108, 109, 115, 144-147, 165, 176
slow fashion, 129, 130, 131, 132, 135, 137, 138, 143-155, 159, 165-168, 173, 175, 177, 178, 179, 180, 181, 185, 186, 193, 195, 209, 213, 216, 231
slow food, 16, 25, 26, 27, 59, 88, 130, 132, 175, 176
slow movement, 16, 25, 26, 27, 28, 30, 33
Slow Research Lab, 27, 28
slowness, 28, 37, 67, 72, 114, 116, 130, 144, 153, 154, 155, 166, 176, 178, 179, 180, 199
Slowtopia, 16, 24, 25, 26, 28, 30, 38
slowversity, 31, 37

W

Z